Wherever you see one of our
someone is having a marvellous

110 luxury narrowboats, with an average age of only 3 years, from 2-12 berths operating from 4 bases, **Alvechurch**, **Birmingham**, **Anderton** and **Gayton**, with a wide choice of canal and river cruising. Short breaks and 10/11 night holidays a speciality.

Write, phone or call for a free colour brochure:
Alvechurch Boat Centres, Scarfield Wharf, Alvechurch, Nr. Birmingham, Worcestershire. B48 7SQ. Tel: 021-445-2909

Pearson's Canal Companion

OXFORD & GRAND UNION

Published by J. M. Pearson & Son, Tatenhill Common, Staffordshire DE13 9RS. Telephone: (0283) 713674
© Michael Pearson – All rights reserved. Second edition 1993. ISBN 0 907864 64 3
Maps by Malcolm Barnes, Cartographer, of Burton-on-Trent. Typesetting and origination by Character Graphics of Taunton
Printed by Clifford Press Ltd., Coventry in association with the Portfolio Press of Barnoldswick

Introduction

IT would be difficult to imagine two canals more different in character than the Oxford and Grand Union, which seem to sit cross-legged on the factory wall of the Midlands, dangling their toes in the Thames. The Oxford, for all its 19th century improvements, is still obviously a first generation canal, tentative in its serpentine course down from Coventry to Oxford, and going, quite literally, to great lengths to avoid the sort of lock-flights and heavy earthworks which later generations of canal builders took in their stride. Exploring it now, one quite easily forgets that it was as significant commercially in its time as the M40 motorway. On the other hand, the Grand Union, modernised in the 1930s, still has about it an atmosphere of trade, even though the best part of twenty-five years have passed since even a modicum of cargoes were carried on it.

THE idea behind combining these two dissimilar waterways in one Canal Companion was to cover the routes radiating from the famous Northamptonshire canal centre of Braunston. The first edition took time to curry favour with 'the trade', but as time went by the reasoning behind our concept became accepted and sales increased. For this new edition, thoroughly re-researched as usual, we have taken a step nearer London by covering the canal south from Cowroast to Berkhamsted, though any further encroachment on the capital must wait for a future edition with more elbow room - like a narrowboat is restricted to the width of Brindley's lock gauge, we have to keep within the confines of our 64 page format. Happy Canalling!

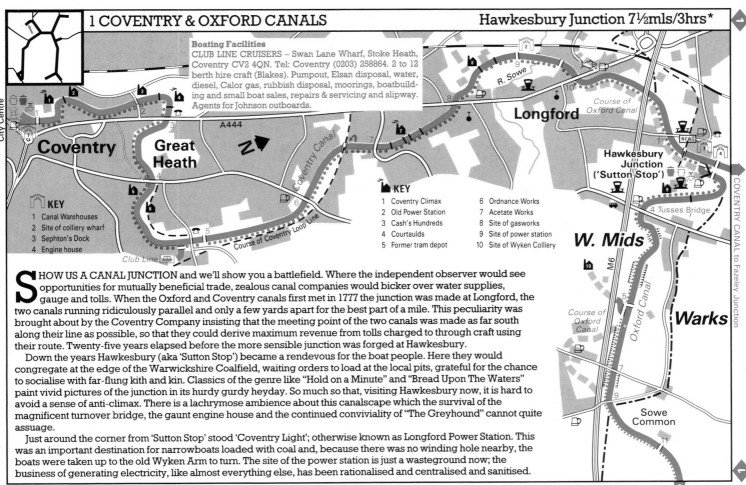

Boating Facilities
CLUB LINE CRUISERS – Swan Lane Wharf, Stoke Heath, Coventry CV2 4QN. Tel: Coventry (0203) 258864. 2 to 12 berth hire craft (Blakes). Pumpout, Elsan disposal, water, diesel, Calor gas, rubbish disposal, moorings, boatbuilding and small boat sales, repairs & servicing and slipway. Agents for Johnson outboards.

KEY
1 Canal Warehouses
2 Site of colliery wharf
3 Sephton's Dock
4 Engine house

KEY
1 Coventry Climax
2 Old Power Station
3 Cash's Hundreds
4 Courtaulds
5 Former tram depot
6 Ordnance Works
7 Acetate Works
8 Site of gasworks
9 Site of power station
10 Site of Wyken Colliery

Coventry · Great Heath · Longford · Hawkesbury Junction ('Sutton Stop') · Course of Oxford Canal · 4 Tusses Bridge · W. Mids · Warks · Sowe Common · Club Line · Course of Coventry Loop Line · Coventry Canal · R. Sowe · City Centre · A444 · COVENTRY CANAL to Fazeley Junction · Oxford Canal

SHOW US A CANAL JUNCTION and we'll show you a battlefield. Where the independent observer would see opportunities for mutually beneficial trade, zealous canal companies would bicker over water supplies, gauge and tolls. When the Oxford and Coventry canals first met in 1777 the junction was made at Longford, the two canals running ridiculously parallel and only a few yards apart for the best part of a mile. This peculiarity was brought about by the Coventry Company insisting that the meeting point of the two canals was made as far south along their line as possible, so that they could derive maximum revenue from tolls charged to through craft using their route. Twenty-five years elapsed before the more sensible junction was forged at Hawkesbury.

Down the years Hawkesbury (aka 'Sutton Stop') became a rendevous for the boat people. Here they would congregate at the edge of the Warwickshire Coalfield, waiting orders to load at the local pits, grateful for the chance to socialise with far-flung kith and kin. Classics of the genre like "Hold on a Minute" and "Bread Upon The Waters" paint vivid pictures of the junction in its hurdy gurdy heyday. So much so that, visiting Hawkesbury now, it is hard to avoid a sense of anti-climax. There is a lachrymose ambience about this canalscape which the survival of the magnificent turnover bridge, the gaunt engine house and the continued conviviality of "The Greyhound" cannot quite assuage.

Just around the corner from 'Sutton Stop' stood 'Coventry Light'; otherwise known as Longford Power Station. This was an important destination for narrowboats loaded with coal and, because there was no winding hole nearby, the boats were taken up to the old Wyken Arm to turn. The site of the power station is just a wasteground now; the business of generating electricity, like almost everything else, has been rationalised and centralised and sanitised.

Figures refer to Map total; allow just 1hr for Oxford Canal section.

For full details of the canals on this page please refer to the SOUTH MIDLANDS Canal Companion.

THE OXFORD CANAL slices through the grain of the countryside like someone cutting an appetizing slice of fruit pie. But instead of oozing blackberry and apple filling, a rural landscape of shallow valleys and modest rises is exposed. And though Coventry looks uncomfortably close on the horizon, the emphasis here is indisputably agricultural, even though two motorways intrude momentarily.

Canal and railway share an embankment near Brinklow, the scene of many well known photographs and paintings depicting narrowboats and steam trains; the tortoise and the hare of 19th century transport. This, though, was not the original course of the canal. Reference to the map will indicate just how tortuous that once was. The embankments and cuttings that characterise the northern section of the Oxford Canal now, date from a rolling programme of 'shortenings' undertaken between 1829 and 1834, which eliminated 15 miles in the course of the canal between Hawkesbury and Braunston. To put this in context one must peel back the layers of time to James Brindley's original survey of the route carried out in 1769. Brindley's well documented predilection for minimising earthworks, resulted in the canal making a 43 mile journey between the Coventry Canal and Napton; a distance of just 15 miles as the crow flies. Like a Royal Walkabout, Brindley also felt that the more places one could visit, the more influence one might have. In some respects he was right. No-one expected canal transport to be fast. Its benefit lay in convenience and reliability. Sections of the old line remained in use for many years serving businesses and wharves already established on its banks. Two examples of this can be seen in the vicinity of Brinklow.

Stretton Stop was formerly a point at which tolls were taken, and the canal narrows appropriately. The scene here is invariably busy and colourful. The arm to Stretton Wharf is used for private moorings. Boaters should take care not to collide with the foot swingbridge which links the towpath side of the canal with the boatyard of Rose Narrowboats.

Fosse Way crosses the canal at bridge 30.

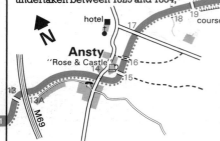

Eating & Drinking

The RAILWAY INN is a basic local overlooking the canal and the site of the village's long lost station. There are several pubs in the village itself, notably THE RAVEN which has changed its allegiance from Ansells to Marstons. Fish & chips are available both sessions daily ex Sun lunch at the far end of the village.

Shopping

The boatyard shop stocks provisions and there is a newsagency/post office and food store in the village as well.

Public Transport

BUSES - Midland Red south operate to/from Rugby via Newbold. Check times on Rugby (0788) 535555.

Boating Facilities

ROSE NARROWBOATS - Stretton-under-Fosse, Rugby, Warks CV23 0PU. Tel: Rugby (0788) 832449. 2 to 10 berth hire craft and day boats in dark red and green livery and named after varieties of rose. Pumpout, Elsan disposal, diesel, petrol (lead free only), Calor gas, servicing & repairs, slipway, chandlery, outboards, gifts, groceries, canal books & maps and payphone.

WARWICKSHIRE NARROWBOATS - address as above. Tel: 832646. Boatbuilders.

Brinklow

The agreeably wide main street is framed by a happy miscellany of building styles and periods. At the edge of the village a pair of rusty iron gates denote the location of a former wharf which lay on the old route of the canal. Past the Perpendicular church, a lane leads up to the motte & bailey outline of a former Norman castle. Altogether one of the best North Oxford Canal villages to visit, but take care of the Fosse Way traffic.

THIS IS PROBABLY the prettiest part of the 'Northern Oxford'. Woodland and farmland mix socially, lingering over a cocktail or two as the canal moves languidly from bridgehole to bridgehole in no apparent hurry to reach Rugby, or anywhere else for that matter.

'Brinklow Arches' were originally a twelve arched aqueduct, carrying the canal over Smite Brook. Brindley and his associate Samuel Simcock had been exasperated by the attitude of a local landowner, who steadfastly refused to let them disturb his pheasant spinneys and fox coverts with their preferred route, which was to have taken the canal higher up the stream to cross it in the vicinity of Newbold Revel. So, reluctantly, the canal builders were forced into the construction of an aqueduct. But this, itself, was replaced by an embankment during the 'modernisations' of the 19th century. Nearby, bridge 32 is a cast iron roving bridge, taking the towpath of the realigned main line over the original course of the canal, which became an arm serving the wharf at Brinklow. The depth of the new cutting is considerable. The engineers were Cubitt

and Vignoles; both men were to make their names with the emerging railways.

At intervals, other sections of the original route join and leave the canal beneath the span of elegant roving bridges cast by the Horseley Iron Works company, whose structures are more commonly associated with the Birmingham Canals. These reedy old arms are, alas, no longer remotely navigable. Furthermore, having long since been subjected to the plough, and traversing private land, they cannot be explored to the extent one might wish. At Newbold-on-Avon, though, those with an enthusiasm for such things can discover the portal of the original tunnel, which penetrated the adjoining hillside at almost right angles to the new one. The original line approached Newbold in a broad arc from the south, meeting the present route at bridge 50, which explains why the two pubs seem nowadays to have no business with the canal. The southern portal of the old tunnel lies at the foot of St Botolph's churchyard. This particular arm was kept profitably in water, because the canal company sold its contents to the London & North Western Railway, who used it to feed nearby water troughs, from which express steam trains could fill their tenders without stopping.

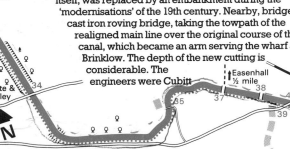

THE SAVING IN DISTANCE achieved by the 19th century improvements to the Oxford Canal is nowhere more apparent than in the vicinity of Rugby. In order to keep to the 300ft contour and minimise earthworks, the original route went wandering off a couple of miles to the north, looking for a convenient point to cross the River Swift. Then, having returned to the outskirts of Rugby via Brownsover, it set off again, this time to cross the Avon near Clifton-on-Dunsmore. Perhaps the contractors were paid by the mile.

The northern outskirts of Rugby are not pretty, but neither are they dull. Retail parks, ring roads, industrial units, housing estates and all the other accumulated junk of the second half of the twentieth century are paraded for the canal traveller's contempt. Cubitt's new route involved a sequence of aqueducts and embankments across the wide valleys of the Swift and Avon which form a confluence just to the south. It makes for a fascinating journey to this day. And there is barely a dull moment as the exits and entrances of the old loops are passed, and you try to piece together the topography of the original canal. There are lost railways to decipher too. The Midland, London & North Western, and Great Central all converged on Rugby, all crossed the Oxford Canal, and all fell foul of Beeching.

A forest of wireless transmitting masts forms a backdrop to the canal centre of Hillmorton. In recent years this has lost its importance as a Section Office and hire base for British Waterways. But, with its trio of duplicated locks, and dignified workshops of the old Oxford Canal Company, it retains a well kept and picturesque canalscape. The three locks raise the canal over 18 feet. The duplicates used to be interconnected, so that each could act as a side pond for the other; a significant saving in water wastage which BW strangely saw fit to abandon in the early Eighties.

KEY
1 Rugby Wharf
2 Clifton Wharf
3 Oxford CC workshops

Rugby
Rugby, its character and facilities, is covered more fully in our "South Midlands & Warwickshire Ring" Canal Companion. Suffice it to say here that though the town centre lies some distance from the canal (a mile and a half at its closest) this interesting and historic town is worth making an effort to see. Mini-buses head frequently for the centre from stops adjacent to bridge 59 near which there are good 24 hour visitor moorings.

Eating & Drinking
BELL & BARGE - canalside bridge 58. Toby Inns grill and bars. There are Chinese and pizza takeaways adjacent to bridge 59.

Shopping
Small supermarket 200 yards south of bridge 59. Tesco store near bridge 58.

Boating Facilities
CLIFTON CRUISERS - Clifton Wharf, Vicarage Hill, Clifton-on-Dunsmore, Rugby, Warks CV23 0DG. Tel: Rugby (0788) 543570. 2 to 7 berth hire craft in red and cream named after Kent and Sussex towns. Bookable through Hoseasons or direct. Good range of facilities - pumpout, gas, etc though not available on Saturdays. Shop with groceries and gifts. WILLOW WREN - Rugby Wharf, Forum Drive, Rugby, Warks CV21 1PB. Tel: Rugby (0788) 562183. 8 to 12 berth hire craft in green and cream colours named after birds, bookable direct. Pumpout, diesel, gas and moorings.

Michael Bee sting! ouch!! shut up shorts as tieing up near Bee Nest!!

5 OXFORD CANAL

Willoughby 4½mls/1½hrs

5

BETWEEN RUGBY AND BRAUNSTON the Oxford Canal plays hopscotch with Warwickshire and Northamptonshire as the border twists back and forth like all good county boundaries, lost in the mists of antiquity, should. This is the old Feldon region - the land south of the Avon - exemplified by a rolling, sparsely wooded countryside, plain to the eye of the casual beholder, but full of interest if you are prepared to delve deeper.

The past stakes a firm claim on this landscape. Remnants of medieval 'ridge & furrow' farming remain obvious in pastures bordering the canal. These patterns, zig-zagging across the fields, were preserved because this formerly arable land - where each ridge represented the individual strip of a peasant farmer - was given over to pasture immediately after the area was enclosed by hawthorn hedges at some time between the 15th and 17th centuries. Such 'clearances' explain the dearth of settlements in the vicinity; whole communities being torn down and peasants sent packing by powerful landowners, to make way for the new more profitable field system.

The canal's past is ever present too. More of its old meanderings can be detected, though long since replaced by lengthy straights. At the north-east end of the shallow cutting by bridge 77, look into the field on the towpath side and you'll see the original bed of the canal, an obvious declivity parallel with the neighbouring hedgerow. More relics of the canal are encountered at the old wharves by bridges 74 and 85; the former's stable block has apparently regained its original use. Between bridges 78 and 79 the towpath is bounded by Oxford Canal Company concrete fence posts bearing the company's initials. The cutting between bridges 83 and 84 has an oddly menacing feel. Not normally susceptible to psychic phenomena, we nevertheless experienced a cold shiver down the spine passing through this tangle of dead trees and putrid water. At twilight bats sweep to and fro in the thickets and we were glad to put the place behind us.

Chronologically much later scar tissue in the landscape is that of the old Great Central Railway. Opened in 1897, it was the last main line to be built in Britain, and the first to close in 1966. We crossed a field to gaze at the former trackbed and disturbed a fox in the cutting. Near bridge 85 a concrete signal post stands stubbornly erect, kindling images of the trains which passed this way - Robinson 'Directors', Gresley 'Sandringhams' and Thompson 'Antelopes' - pounding through the Shires on their way to the capital from Lancashire, Yorkshire and the East Midlands.

Eating & Drinking
THE OLD ROYAL OAK - canalside bridge 73. Popular refurbished free house offering a good range of bar meals. Children catered for, garden and payphone.

Boating Facilities
CLUB LINE - Hillmorton Wharf, Crick Road. Tel: Rugby (0788) 577300. Moorings, drydock, pumpout and other boating facilities, plus souvenir shop.

A428

N

A - 1845 or later
D - 1010?

Club Line
'Old Royal Oak'

74
73
former wharf
& stables

LNWR Birmingham London

Warks

75

76

Northants

Rugby

Former course of Oxford Canal

77

78

M45

79

80

Barby Wood Farm

81   82

83   84

85
former wharf

'ridge & furrow'

87

Great Central Railway

Warks

A45

6

Willoughby   5

Coventry

9

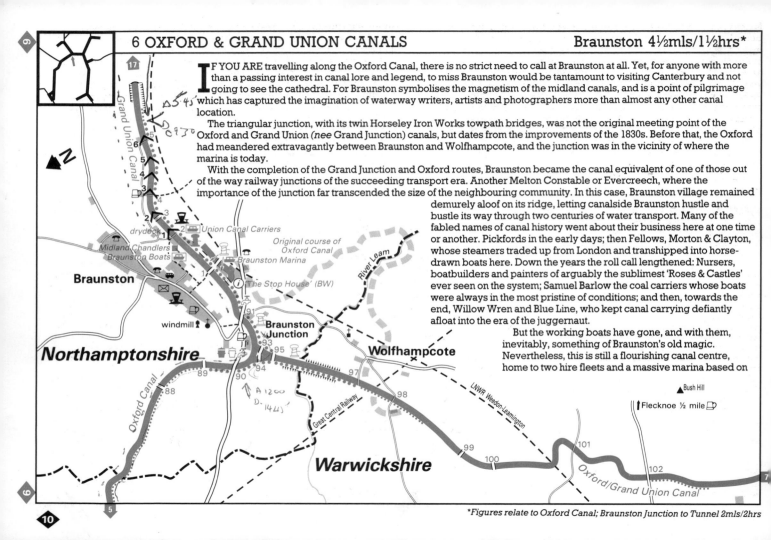

IF YOU ARE travelling along the Oxford Canal, there is no strict need to call at Braunston at all. Yet, for anyone with more than a passing interest in canal lore and legend, to miss Braunston would be tantamount to visiting Canterbury and not going to see the cathedral. For Braunston symbolises the magnetism of the midland canals, and is a point of pilgrimage which has captured the imagination of waterway writers, artists and photographers more than almost any other canal location.

The triangular junction, with its twin Horseley Iron Works towpath bridges, was not the original meeting point of the Oxford and Grand Union (*nee* Grand Junction) canals, but dates from the improvements of the 1830s. Before that, the Oxford had meandered extravagantly between Braunston and Wolfhampcote, and the junction was in the vicinity of where the marina is today.

With the completion of the Grand Junction and Oxford routes, Braunston became the canal equivalent of one of those out of the way railway junctions of the succeeding transport era. Another Melton Constable or Evercreech, where the importance of the junction far transcended the size of the neighbouring community. In this case, Braunston village remained demurely aloof on its ridge, letting canalside Braunston hustle and bustle its way through two centuries of water transport. Many of the fabled names of canal history went about their business here at one time or another. Pickfords in the early days; then Fellows, Morton & Clayton, whose steamers traded up from London and transhipped into horse-drawn boats here. Down the years the roll call lengthened: Nursers, boatbuilders and painters of arguably the sublimest 'Roses & Castles' ever seen on the system; Samuel Barlow the coal carriers whose boats were always in the most pristine of conditions; and then, towards the end, Willow Wren and Blue Line, who kept canal carrying defiantly afloat into the era of the juggernaut.

But the working boats have gone, and with them, inevitably, something of Braunston's old magic. Nevertheless, this is still a flourishing canal centre, home to two hire fleets and a massive marina based on

Map labels

Grand Union Canal

Braunston

drydeck

Midland Chandlers
Braunston Boats

Union Canal Carriers

Original course of
Oxford Canal

River Leam

Braunston Marina

'The Stop House' (BW)

windmill

Northamptonshire

Braunston Junction

Wolfhampcote

Oxford Canal

Great Central Railway

Warwickshire

LNWR Weedon-Leamington

Bush Hill

Flecknoe ½ mile

Oxford/Grand Union Canal

*Figures relate to Oxford Canal; Braunston Junction to Tunnel 2mls/2hrs

former reservoirs. Wander along the towpath and you'll see new boats being built, old ones restored, and a regular stream of traffic up and down the locks, and it only takes the aroma of a charcoal stove, the beat of a Bolinder, or the rattle of ratchets in the twilight of an Autumn afternoon to conjure up the old atmosphere, and make you glad you came. British Waterways have refurbished the former 'Stop House' as their area office, and it includes an exhibition room with a changing cycle of interesting displays devoted to the canal's history. Through the toll window itself, the wax work (or is it?) figure of the night clerk can be seen writing in his ledger by candle light.

The five mile section between Braunston and Napton is interesting scenically and historically. It is a thoroughly remote length of canal; the countryside falling flatly away to the north-west, but climbing abruptly to a notable ridge in the opposite direction. There are ghosts everywhere: old reedy loops of canal, abandoned railways, lost villages and 'friendless' churches. and, Napton side of Wolfhampcote, no towpath worthy of the name.

When the Grand Union Canal was formed in 1929, there remained a gap between its former Grand Junction (London-Braunston) and Warwick & Napton constituents which belonged to the Oxford Canal. Knowing a good thing when they saw it, the Oxford company kindly allowed the Grand Union to pick up the tab for a programme of dredging and concrete banking, at the same time continuing to extract tolls from them until Nationalisation. A phenomenon relating to this 'joint' length is that boats travelling between the Midlands and the South, via either the Oxford or Grand Union, pass each other going in the opposite direction.

Braunston

Village Braunston straddles its ridge, 400 feet up on the slopes of the Northamptonshire uplands. Enclosed fields, still bearing the pattern of ridge & furrow, distil the spirit of the Middle Ages. Sauntering along the High Street from the village green to the tall spired church, one encounters a mixture of stone and brick buildings, including a sail-less and now residential windmill and a 17th century manor house. At the foot of a long hill the A45 crosses the canal. This was the Chester turnpike road which became part of Telford's route from London to Holyhead. There was a tollhouse here at the foot of the winding and precipitous descent from Daventry. During the second world war a considerable number of evacuees were billeted in the village, which had only just been put on the electricity mains, and Braunston continues to evoke a timeless air which has much to commend it.

Eating & Drinking

BOATMAN HOTEL - canalside near junction. Bar and restaurant meals in waterside pub long ago disfigured by a Mississippi steamboat style extension.
OLD PLOUGH - High Street. GBG recommended pub up in the village. Bar food and Ansells beer. Table skittles. Families catered for.

ADMIRAL NELSON - canalside bridge 4. Ruddles, bar meals, garden, skittles. (Children only welcome inside if eating full meal.)

Shopping

Enticing aromas issue from the village bakery (Goodness Foods). A few doors along, Gurney's well stocked general store, newsagency and off licence caters for most needs. It is open daily but early closes on Mondays and Sundays. Elsewhere in High Street there is a butcher and post office (half day Wed). Down by the canal groceries are obtainable from THE BOAT SHOP alongside bottom lock, a delightful shop dealing in canal gifts and souvenirs too.

Public Transport

BUSES - Geoff Amos Coaches to/from Rugby and Daventry. Tel: Daventry (0327) 702181. Reasonably frequent Mon-Sat service useful for towpath walks between Rugby and Braunston.

Boating Facilities

BRAUNSTON BOATS - Bottom Lock, Braunston, Daventry, Northants NN11 7HL. Tel: Rugby (0788) 891079 or 541020. 2 to 12 berth hire craft in predominently green livery named mostly after canal related villages. Bookable direct or through Blakes. Hire fleet includes "Binnenschip", a scaled-down Dutch barge. Pumpout, diesel, gas, moorings and surveys.
BRAUNSTON MARINA - Braunston, Daventry, Northants NN11 7JH. Tel: Rugby (0788) 891373. Diesel, Calor gas, moorings, sales & brokerage, drydock DIY facilities, slipway, repairs & servicing, traditional signwriting and chandlery.
UNION CANAL CARRIERS - Canal Side, Little Braunston, Daventry, Northants NN11 7HJ. Tel: Rugby (0788) 890784. 2 to 12 berth hire craft in dark green colours named after hills. Traditional camping boats as well. Book direct. Pumpout, diesel, Shell and Calor gas, repairs & servicing, fitting-out, drydock with DIY facilities. 24 hour breakdown service.
MIDLAND CHANDLERS - Bottom Lock, Braunston. Tel: Rugby (0788) 891401.

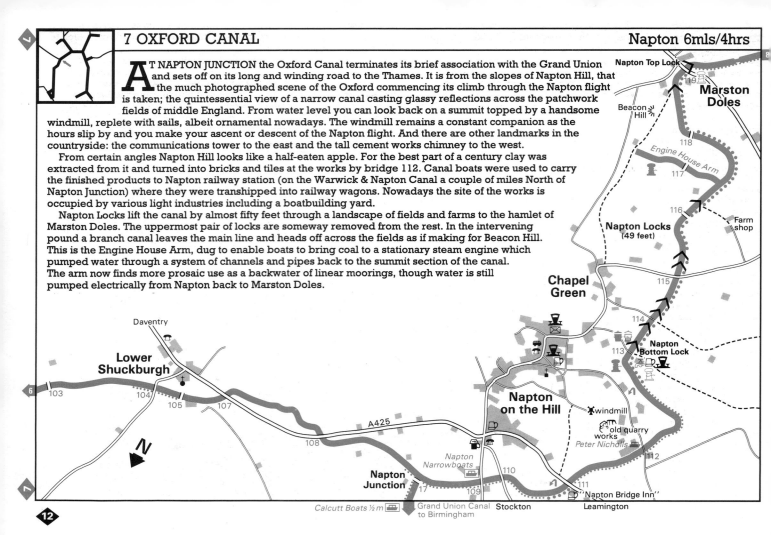

AT NAPTON JUNCTION the Oxford Canal terminates its brief association with the Grand Union and sets off on its long and winding road to the Thames. It is from the slopes of Napton Hill, that the much photographed scene of the Oxford commencing its climb through the Napton flight is taken; the quintessential view of a narrow canal casting glassy reflections across the patchwork fields of middle England. From water level you can look back on a summit topped by a handsome windmill, replete with sails, albeit ornamental nowadays. The windmill remains a constant companion as the hours slip by and you make your ascent or descent of the Napton flight. And there are other landmarks in the countryside: the communications tower to the east and the tall cement works chimney to the west.

From certain angles Napton Hill looks like a half-eaten apple. For the best part of a century clay was extracted from it and turned into bricks and tiles at the works by bridge 112. Canal boats were used to carry the finished products to Napton railway station (on the Warwick & Napton Canal a couple of miles North of Napton Junction) where they were transhipped into railway wagons. Nowadays the site of the works is occupied by various light industries including a boatbuilding yard.

Napton Locks lift the canal by almost fifty feet through a landscape of fields and farms to the hamlet of Marston Doles. The uppermost pair of locks are someway removed from the rest. In the intervening pound a branch canal leaves the main line and heads off across the fields as if making for Beacon Hill. This is the Engine House Arm, dug to enable boats to bring coal to a stationary steam engine which pumped water through a system of channels and pipes back to the summit section of the canal. The arm now finds more prosaic use as a backwater of linear moorings, though water is still pumped electrically from Napton back to Marston Doles.

Napton Top Lock

119

Marston Doles

Beacon Hill

Engine House Arm

118

117

116

Farm shop

Napton Locks (49 feet)

115

114

Napton Bottom Lock

113

Chapel Green

Daventry

Lower Shuckburgh

103

104

105

107

108

A425

Napton on the Hill

✠ windmill

old quarry works

Peter Nicholls

112

110

111

Napton Narrowboats

Napton Junction

17

109

"Napton Bridge Inn"

Leamington

Calcutt Boats ½ m → Grand Union Canal to Birmingham **Stockton**

Napton basks in the sunshine on its south-facing hill. Its street pattern takes some fathoming, but there is lots of green space between the houses and even the modern developments seem to dovetail neatly in. You can climb towards the windmill by a footpath from bridge 111, but it is a private residence now and not open to the public.

Eating & Drinking
THE NAPTON BRIDGE INN - canalside bridge 111. Bar and restaurant food.
THE FOLLY INN - adjacent bridge 113. Once known as the 'Bull & Butcher', and relicenced in 1990 after many years in the wilderness, this is a welcoming pub offering home made food including afternoon teas during the summer. Nice big garden and adjoining gift shop.

Shopping
Useful provisions outlets include the lock-keeper's cottage at Napton Bottom Lock and the Farm Shop reached from the lock near bridge 116. The village itself has two stores. Wednesday is half day at the post office.

Public Transport
BUSES - Midland Red South to/from Leamington Spa. Tel: Rugby (0788) 535555.

Boating Facilities
NAPTON NARROWBOATS - Napton Marina, Stockton, Rugby, Warks CV23 8HX. Tel: Southam (0926) 813644. 2 to 10 berth hire craft in grey/blue livery named after birds prefixed by canal towns and villages. Bookable direct or through Hoseasons. Pumpout, Elsan and refuse disposal, water, diesel, Shell gas, moorings, slipway, wetdock, laundry facilities, shop with gifts, groceries and off licence.
CALCUTT BOATS - Stockton, Rugby, Warks CV23 8HX. Tel: Southam (0926) 813757. 2 to 9 berth hire craft in white and green livery named after wild flowers; bookable direct or through Hoseasons. Pumpout, Elsan disposal, water, diesel, Calor gas, moorings, repairs & servicing, slipway, drydock, boatbuilding, sales & brokerage, crane/lift-out facilities, shop with groceries, gifts, off licence, chandlery and payphone.

Just a huddle of houses, a pub and a garage, on the busy A423. The village itself is a mile and a half beyond the railway. The GEORGE & DRAGON (canalside bridge 136) is a popular boaters watering-hole offering bar and restaurant food. The beer is Bass and M&B, there's a pool table in the public bar and a garden with resident menagerie. The pub also operate the adjoining WHARF STORES, open throughout the cruising season for groceries, newspapers and gifts. Significantly, this is the third pub we came across on our research trips for this edition diversifying into shop-keeping; shades of Ireland?

Boating Facilities
COWROAST - Fenny Marina, Fenny Compton, Warwickshire CV33 0XD. Tel: Fenny (0295) 770461. Pumpout, diesel, water, Elsan & rubbish disposal, Calor gas, moorings, repairs & servicing, fitting-out, sales & brokerage, wet-dock, chandlery, gifts & books, groceries.

"Napton Bottom.

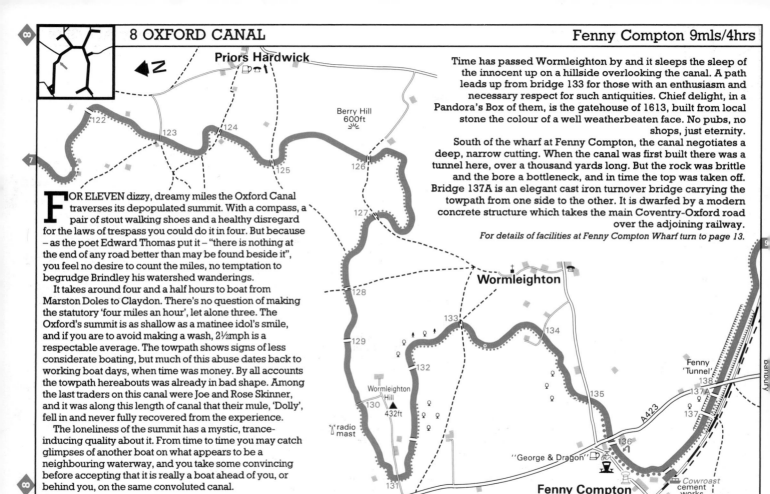

Priors Hardwick

Berry Hill 600ft

Time has passed Wormleighton by and it sleeps the sleep of the innocent up on a hillside overlooking the canal. A path leads up from bridge 133 for those with an enthusiasm and necessary respect for such antiquities. Chief delight, in a Pandora's Box of them, is the gatehouse of 1613, built from local stone the colour of a well weatherbeaten face. No pubs, no shops, just eternity.

South of the wharf at Fenny Compton, the canal negotiates a deep, narrow cutting. When the canal was first built there was a tunnel here, over a thousand yards long. But the rock was brittle and the bore a bottleneck, and in time the top was taken off. Bridge 137A is an elegant cast iron turnover bridge carrying the towpath from one side to the other. It is dwarfed by a modern concrete structure which takes the main Coventry-Oxford road over the adjoining railway.

For details of facilities at Fenny Compton Wharf turn to page 13.

F OR ELEVEN dizzy, dreamy miles the Oxford Canal traverses its depopulated summit. With a compass, a pair of stout walking shoes and a healthy disregard for the laws of trespass you could do it in four. But because – as the poet Edward Thomas put it – "there is nothing at the end of any road better than may be found beside it", you feel no desire to count the miles, no temptation to begrudge Brindley his watershed wanderings.

It takes around four and a half hours to boat from Marston Doles to Claydon. There's no question of making the statutory 'four miles an hour', let alone three. The Oxford's summit is as shallow as a matinee idol's smile, and if you are to avoid making a wash, 2½mph is a respectable average. The towpath shows signs of less considerate boating, but much of this abuse dates back to working boat days, when time was money. By all accounts the towpath hereabouts was already in bad shape. Among the last traders on this canal were Joe and Rose Skinner, and it was along this length of canal that their mule, 'Dolly', fell in and never fully recovered from the experience.

The loneliness of the summit has a mystic, trance-inducing quality about it. From time to time you may catch glimpses of another boat on what appears to be a neighbouring waterway, and you take some convincing before accepting that it is really a boat ahead of you, or behind you, on the same convoluted canal.

Wormleighton

Wormleighton Hill
432ft

radio mast

Fenny 'Tunnel'

A423

"George & Dragon"

Fenny Compton

Cowroast cement works

Coventry

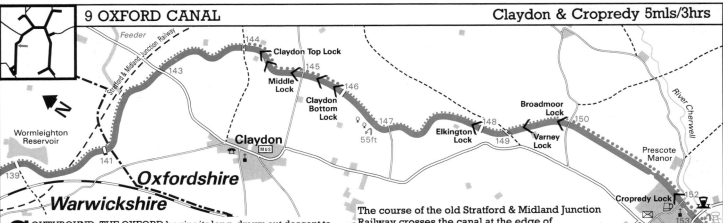

Claydon Top Lock

Middle Lock

Claydon Bottom Lock

Broadmoor Lock

Elkington Lock

Varney Lock

Wormleighton Reservoir

Claydon
MUS

Oxfordshire

Warwickshire

River Cherwell

Prescote Manor

Cropredy Lock

Cropredy

Feeder

55ft

SOUTHBOUND, THE OXFORD begins its long, drawn out descent to the Thames. Northwards, Claydon marks the start of the summit section; no more locks to work for the best part of 5 hours!

Wormleighton, Boddington and Clattercote are not, as you might assume, a firm of Banbury solicitors, but rather the three reservoirs which feed the Oxford Canal. Water shortages have always been a problem on this waterway and at times the density of pleasure boat traffic exacerbates this, forcing British Waterways to restrict the opening hours of the locks; a practice of dubious effect which, arguably, concentrates useage rather than reducing it; though at least it allows staff to ensure that no careless boaters leave paddles up overnight. Apparently the summit was dug deliberately deeper than the rest of the canal in order to retain as much water as it could, though it is obvious that this facility no longer exists.

Bridge 141 straddles the county boundary and is the northernmost of the characteristic draw bridges synonymous with this canal. These structures are simplicity defined, consisting of no more than a pair of shallow brick abutments, a platform and two hefty timber balance beams set at 45 degrees when the bridge is closed to boats, or flat against the nettles when, as is often the case, they are left open. Seen from afar, they punctuate the Oxford Canal's passage through the Cherwell Valley, as homogeneous with this landscape as the pollarded willows of its watermeadows and the oolite stonework of its villages.

The course of the old Stratford & Midland Junction Railway crosses the canal at the edge of Wormleighton Reservoir. One of those forgotten little railways whose high hopes were never realised, it became disparagingly, but affectionately known as the 'Slow, Mouldy and Jolting'. Tom Rolt loved the unhurried progress of its trains: their "Slow, panting climbs, and swift, swaying descents" across the Northampton Uplands.

At Claydon the Oxford Canal company built workshops and stables beside the top lock. This would have been a busy spot in the heyday of the canal - now it's as quiet as the grave. Three isolated locks interrupt the canal's otherwise uneventful progress between Claydon and Cropredy. Above Elkington Lock there is a small holding where you may be able to obtain fresh eggs. A company specialising in the maintenance and repair of wooden boats occupies a site beside Broadmoor Lock.

A well surfaced towpath leads to Cropredy where horses graze in the waterside pastures and pigs frolic in the muddy margins of the canal. The old wharf is used by Banbury Canoe Club, though the former toll office and gauging narrows recall a busier past. The lock cottage is charming, making you regret all the more the loss of so many of the others along this canal. 48 hour visitor moorings are available between bridges 152 and 153

10

9

Claydon

The John O' Groats of Oxfordshire - in other words the county's most northerly village - Claydon is shopless and publess and windswept, but it is worth trudging up from the canal to visit THE GRANARY MUSEUM. Retired farmer, Andrew Fox, began collecting - and by his own admission, hoarding - articles that the rest of us throw far too easily nearly fifty years ago. Items on display range from old cash registers to pre-war tractors, and there is even a 1912 Aveling-Porter steam road roller. Several old shops from Banbury, demolished to make way for a new road, have been re-erected in the timeless sanctuary of the farm's former cowsheds and barns. Being privately owned, the museum avoids the formality which can afflict larger establishments. There are no organised opening times and there is no fixed admission fee. If Mr Fox is in, you are welcomed. The museum also includes a nicely stocked gift shop, whilst Mr Fox's daughter does coffees and cream teas at her house across the road.

Cropredy

Villages like Cropredy don't have a history, they have a heartbeat. The passage of time seems irrelevant, the centuries foreshorten. There was a Civil War battle here in 1644, but to hear the villagers talk it might have been yesterday. Ten thousand men took part and some of the clobber they left behind - helmets, bayonets and cannon balls - is on display in the church, along with a pre-Reformation brass lectern which was apparently submerged in the Cherwell safe from the maurading Puritans. Cropredy's other claim to fame is that it is the scene of folk group "Fairport Convention's" annual re-union concert. The "Brasenose Inn" featured on the cover of one of the group's albums.

Eating & Drinking
THE RED LION - adjacent bridge 152. Thatched village inn visited by Temple Thurston, L.T.C. Rolt and now us. Seems to have lost little of its charm. The sunlight still shines from across the neighbouring churchyard and glints on your pint of Wadworth 6X. Good range of food lunchtimes and evenings: families welcome.
BRASENOSE INN - 300 yards west of bridge 153. M&B, Bass, bar and restaurant meals.

Shopping
BRIDGE STORES by bridge 153 is open daily until late but am only on Sundays. It stocks groceries, wines & spirits, newspapers, gifts and Calor gas. Deeper into the village you'll come upon a craft shop and post office (EC Wed & Sat).

Public Transport
BUSES - Midland Red services to/from Banbury Mon-Sat, but only three or four each way. Tel: Banbury 253451.

Banbury

Since the opening of the M40 motorway, Banbury seems to have re-invented itself, smartened up its act, pedestrianised its thoroughfares, and cleaned up its canalside. It may still come as an unwelcome intrusion to the otherwise rural character of the Oxford Canal, but it isn't half useful for laying on stores, replenishing the wallet and stocking up on local tourist literature at the excellent TIC. Furthermore, the 'new' Banbury has more pride in its appearance than its dowdy predecessor. The streets appear cleaner and more revealing of the pleasant architecture surviving from its days as a bustling country town. Our favourite building is the former corn factors by the market place, its upper storey a signwritten reminder of Banbury's importance as an agricultural centre, the only pity is that the ground floor is now occupied by a building society, but perhaps that says something about the age in which we live and its twisted priorities. Neither has Banbury forgotten its niche in the pantheon of nursery rhymes, and a replica cross, put up by the Victorians following removal of the original by a Puritan mob in 1600, can still be seen at the southern end of The Horsefair.

Eating & Drinking
REINE DEER INN – Parsons Street. Town centre 16th century inn refurbished in 1993. Food freshly made on the premises. Hook Norton ales. Teas in the 'Globe Room' where Cromwell planned his strategy for the Battle of Edgehill.

Shopping
Marks & Spencer have a good store within a stone's throw of the canal opposite the bus park. Shopping in the town is generally a pleasant experience, all the well known 'High Street' names are here, plus some interesting individual retailers as well. Early closing takes place on Tuesdays when the town really does seem to empty. Thursday and Saturday are the market days. MALCOLM'S BAKERY near the TIC makes Banbury Cakes to an authentic recipe.

Things to Do
BANBURY MUSEUM & TOURIST INFORMATION - The Horsefair, Banbury. Tel: Banbury (0295) 259855. One of the best TIC's we've ever come across. Well stocked, helpful staff, light refreshments; even stocks the Canal Companions!
SPICEBALL PARK SPORTS CENTRE - handily placed canalside complex of swimming pools, squash courts, saunas etc.

Public Transport
BUSES - Midland Red services throughout the area. Tel: Banbury (0295) 253451.
TRAINS - services to/from Birmingham, Oxford & London. Tel: Oxford (0865) 722333.

Boating Facilities
SOVEREIGN NARROWBOATS - Compton Road, Banbury OX16 8AA. Tel: Banbury (0295) 275657. 2 to 8 berth hire craft in the red, white and blue of the old Grand Union Canal Carrying Co., named after kings and bookable direct. Pumpout, diesel, Calor gas, long term moorings, repairs & servicing.
MORSE MARINE - Tel: Banbury (0295) 261221. Occupies former Tooley boat dock. Boatbuilding and general services.
FRIENDSHIP CRUISES - public & charter trips. Tel: Banbury 250719.

AT CROPREDY the Oxford Canal first makes eye contact with the River Cherwell, but their's is an affair which makes many twists and turns before consumation finally takes place. In the early years of the century the canal company acquired Cropredy Mill and used the mill stream to provide the canal with water. Up on the hillside above Slat Mill lock stands Williamscot House which dates from the 16th century. With the river and railway as companions, the canal progresses uneventfully through a rural landscape to the outskirts of Banbury. By Hardwick Lock the M40 motorway makes its northernmost crossing of the canal.

Banbury sits like an unfortunate bruise on the otherwise peaches and cream complexion of the 'Southern Oxford'. For two or three turgid miles the picturesque images normally associated with this canal are invaded by factories, ring-roads, and urban sprawl. Given this ugly environment, it is not surprising that Banbury's canal acquired a reputation for hooliganism. Thankfully, though, this seems to have abated. Probably the development of waterside retirement homes, the construction of a new inner relief road and the welcome introduction of a hire base have combined to swing the pendulum away from seediness in the general direction of well-being.

Back in the fifties, Banbury was still the centre for a certain amount of trade on the Oxford Canal. 'Dolly' brought *Friendship* down here with coal; Thomas Clayton's traded to the tar works; and British Waterways' boats carried occasional cargoes of timber to the Co-op wharf. Up until this time Banbury supported its own canal community who were wont to congregate at a spit & sawdust pub called "The Struggler". Rolt immortalised it in his "Inland Waterways of England". The pub and the canal wharf itself were demolished by the local council in 1962, and they added insult to injury by building the bus park on the site. Rolt got to know Banbury and its environs well while he waited in 1939 for Tooleys to complete the docking and fitting-out of *Cressy* prior to its cruise through the canals of the Midlands and North-west so vividly described in his famous book "Narrow Boat".

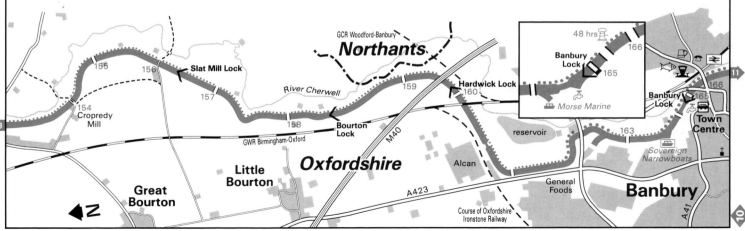

Oxon / Northants

GWR Birmingham-Oxford

Kings Sutton

Grants Lock
9ft 6ins

River Cherwell

works

174

175

173

176

177

179

172

M40

Kings Sutton Lock
10ft 8ins

170 171

Twyford Wharf

181

182

168

"Banbury Fringe Walk"

To Bodicote ½ mile

Adderbury 1 mile

Banbury & Cheltenham Railway

IT TAKES THE canal a bit of while to shake off the suburbs of Banbury, but once it has it resumes its charming passage through the Cherwell Valley like a rambler, journeying not so much with an end in view, but travelling hopefully for the sheer enjoyment of it all. Draw bridges begin to abound; their functional looks disguising the economy of construction which lay behind their design. Another worthwhile saving was the provision of single bottom gates to each lock chamber as opposed to the more usual mitred pairs found north of Banbury.

The spire of King's Sutton church soars above the watermeadows and keeps you company for an hour or two. A white plume of smoke issues from the fertilizer works at Twyford Mill. The river forms the county boundary hereabouts, and so the village itself lies in Northamptonshire. Kings Sutton Lock is delightful. The keeper's cottage is simply built of brick with stone facing. On the opposite bank stands a former blacksmith's forge and stable block. Someone's had the good taste to erect what looks like the old lettering from the village station, so you can't mistake which lock *this* is.

South of here the canal momentarily sheds its man-made character. The branches of pollarded willows hang caressingly over the water and poplars whisper in the breeze as a belt of woodland is encountered.

Into this exquisite landscape the motorway comes like a kick in the groin. When it was being constructed the "Sunday Times" ran a sequence of photographs, taken from the neighbouring hillside and looking out over the valley towards King's Sutton. It was a sobering illustration of the assassination of the Oxfordshire landscape, as hideous in its way as the sort of photographs they show of bodies in the streets after a military coup. According to the Department of Transport the viability of new road schemes is tested on a cost benefit basis. Yes, we know: for the road lobby's benefit at the countryside's cost.

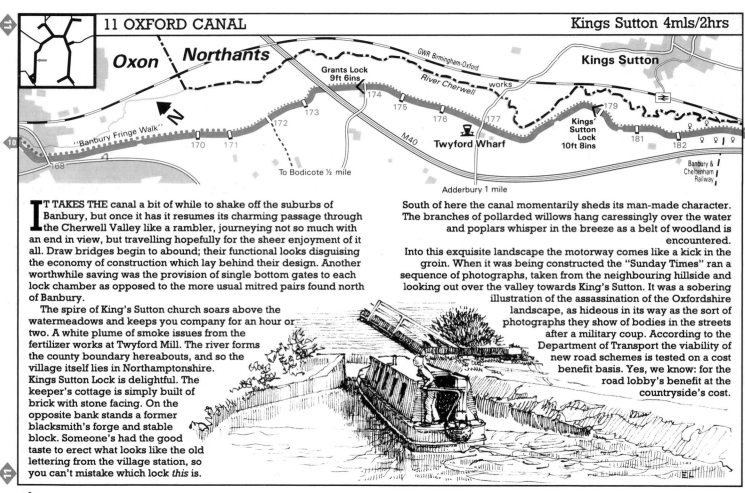

PASSING BRIEFLY into Northamptonshire, the canal shares much of this part of its journey with the adjoining railway, but loses little of its tranquility in the process. After having played coquettishly with the canal's affections since Banbury, the River Cherwell flirts outrageously with it below Nell Bridge, actually having the affrontery to cross it on the level just above Aynho Weir Lock. The lock here is shallow and diamond shaped. The next lock down at Somerton was so deep that extra capacity had to be built into this one to provide an equivalent amount of water.

Aynho railway junction marks the northern end of the Great Western Railway's 'cut off' route, opened in 1910 to shorten their long winded route from London to Birmingham by way of Oxford. It reduced the distance by almost twenty miles and gave the GWR a real boost in their competition with the LNWR for traffic between the first and second cities of the land.

Aynho Canal Wharf is remarkably attractive. Its redbrick wharf buildings remain largely intact, being used as a hire base and canal shop. South of this point the canal becomes lost in the wilds again, passing another old wharf which formerly served the little village of Souldern. If you look closely at bridge 192, you will see the number 150 engraved on its keystone. The whole sequence of bridge numbers was re-numbered on the canal following the improvements 'up north' in the 1840s. In the vicinity of Heyford one or two bridges retain single numbers which relate to the separate numbering of

stone built bridges from an earlier period.

Somerton Deep Lock is - well, very deep. In fact it vies with Tardebigge Top Lock on the Worcester & Birmingham Canal as being the deepest narrowbeam chamber on the canal system. Certainly the steerer's eye view of things, when the lock is empty, is reminiscent of an elephant trap. Goodness knows what the single-handed captains of working boats made of it in the past. Tom Foxon hints at his method in his book,"Number One", also relating how it was his habit to swap lumps of coal with the lock-keeper and his wife in exchange for fresh laid eggs and a rabbit or two. Those were the days!

Aynho Wharf

Eating & Drinking

GREAT WESTERN ARMS – adjacent bridge 190. Hook Norton, bar meals, families catered for, garden. Pleasant stone built pub named after the adjoining railway and suitably decorated with ephemera and artefacts. After you've had a drink or two go and look at the attractive old station building. Handy coal merchant for the solid fuel brigade.

Boating Facilities

ANGLO WELSH - Station Road, Aynho, Banbury, Oxon OX17 3BP. Tel: Banbury (0869) 38483. 2 to 10 berth hire craft bookable from Market Harborough head office on MH (0858) 466910. Pumpout, diesel, water, refuse disposal, Shell gas, moorings, repairs & servicing, boatbuilding & fitting-out, and excellent shop dealing in books, gifts and groceries.

CANAL, RIVER AND RAILWAY saunter along the valley floor, but the roads keep cautiously to the shoulders of the hills. When the Cherwell bursts its banks, the escaping water forms an inland sea from one edge of the valley to the other, and wildfowl find this an attractive wintering ground. In spring the meadows seem full of lapwings carrying out their dizzy courtship. Between Somerton and Heyford the canal assumes the character of a river. The towpath loses its formality, becoming more of a track through the adjoining fields. Pollarded willows line the canal's banks, just like they do the Cherwell's. Seen from a passing train, it is often difficult to tell immediately which is which.

The pound between Heyford Common and Allen's locks looks idyllic enough, but it is not somewhere to linger unless you have an enthusiasm for military aircraft, for up on the hillside to the east lies a military airfield and the decibel levels hereabouts can be exceedingly high. Whether or not you find the aircraft intrusive, they emphasise – just as the new motorway does to the north of here – the fragile nature of the Cherwell Valley's beauty and how much the Oxford Canal's charm relies on the continued survival of the local countryside.

Green issues and politics apart, the aerodrome has an interesting history dating back to its opening as a small RAF station during the First World War. During the last war it was used by Bomber Command. The Americans took over in 1950 and it has become one of their most important fighter bases. You won't have ventured far into Upper Heyford without hearing the strident accents of Kansas and Kentucky mixed with the more dulcet tones of East Oxfordshire.

Between the two Heyfords the canal arcs through a belt of woodland. There are glimpses of a gorgeous cluster of stone buildings – a church, a manor house and a 15th century tithe barn – below Allen's Lock, and of a mill adorned with red creeper near bridge 205; this latter is more hefty than the usual Oxford drawbridges, apparently at some time the miller had a steam traction engine which somewhat exceeded the recommended weight limit laid down for these bridges. Heyford Wharf is almost a mirror image of the one at Aynho, having found an appropriate new lease of life as a hire base, but on this occasion the wharf buildings were built from local stone.

The Heyfords

Two soporific villages built largely from the creamy-coloured local stone. The 'peace dividend' has resulted in a welcome reduction in aircraft noise, and the USAF base at Upper Heyford is earmarked for a reduction to 'standby' status in 1994.

Eating & Drinking

THE BELL - Market Square, Lower Heyford. Charming and peaceful 16th century inn overlooking the village's former market place. Nice cool, shadowy, unrefurbished, and above all *quiet* interior, together with a range of good beers (Adnams, Burton Ale etc) make this a pleasant venue after a hard day on the canal. Families catered for but food limited to snacks.

THREE HORSESHOES - Upper Heyford. Friendly pub which doubles as the village shop; wide range of meals usually available. Also worth trying is THE BARLEY MOW, Fullers beers.

Shopping

Small post office stores tucked away in Lower Heyford (consult map for location). Newspapers and modest groceries. Open daily, am only Sat & Sun. Upper Heyford now has a shop as an annex to the

Boating Facilities

OXFORDSHIRE NARROWBOATS - Station Road, Lower Heyford, Oxon OX5 3PD. Tel: Steeple Aston (0869) 40348. 2 to 12 berth hire craft in blue and yellow colours bookable direct or through Hoseasons. Pumpout, diesel, refuse disposal, moorings, repairs & servicing, drydock, DIY facilities, chandlery, gifts, boat painting and boat hoist.

Map labels: Somerton, flight path, USAF Airfield, Upper Heyford, Allen's Lock 5ft, River Cherwell, mill, Lower Heyford, Heyford Common Lock 7ft 2ins, To Steeple Aston ½ mile, "Three Horseshoes" pub, Oxfordshire Narrowboats, The Cleeves, Rousham Park, GWR Birmingham-Oxford, pipe, B4030. Bridge numbers: 196, 198, 199, 200, 201, 202, 203, 204, 205, 206, 207. Panel numbers: 12, 13, 14.

THE OXFORD CANAL is arguably at its loveliest between Heyford and Thrupp. It drifts through the delicious landscape of the Cherwell Valley like something out of the slow heart of a piano concerto, weaving romantic melodies with the harmony of birdsong and the rhythm of the wind in the reedbeds.

At Northbrook the canal bridge abuts a much older structure spanning the river. This carried a packhorse way across the Cherwell centuries before the canal was even thought of. A mile or two to the south lies the course of the Roman's *Akeman Street* which connected Cirencester with St Alban's. Immediately south of the course of the Roman road, the canal passes through a dark, emerald tunnel of overhanging trees, which retains an almost primeval quality that the legions must have been familiar, if not exactly at ease, with.

In the heart of the wood lie the enigmatic ruins of an old cement works. The canal formed the only practical access to and from the site. Coal, sand and gypsum were brought in by boat and cement taken out, much of it travelling only as far as Enslow where it was transhipped to rail. The works closed in 1927, production being taken up at a new plant with rail access on the hillside above Baker's Lock; though this in turn has become virtually disused.

There used to be a boatman's pub called "The Three Pigeon's" by bridge

213; hence the name of the adjoining lock. It must have been a welcome resort for the thirsty cement workers, but a long time has past since the last pint was supped, though the building remains as a private residence, as does another of the Cherwell's former mills standing nearby. Paths lead from Pigeon's Lock to the villages of Tackley to the west and Kirtlington to the east.

Just beneath the railway bridge at Enslow you can see old mooring rings set in the wall and the scars of unloading apparatus where the cement was transhipped from boats into railway wagons. Transport of a different era is lined up in the haulage company's yard on the opposite bank: a fine array of Foden lorries with names like *Enslow Monarch* and *Enslow Lady.*

Below Baker's Lock comes that act of consummation between the canal and the river which we anticipated long ago at Cropredy. For the best part of a mile the two waterways are one in a charming interlude which sees them zig-zagging, arm in arm down to Shipton Weir Lock. When the Cherwell is in flood this can be a hair-raising journey for the boater. At such times navigation downstream will have all the characteristics of a theme park log flume, whilst whether or not you can make any headway upstream will depend largely upon the power output of your boat's engine.

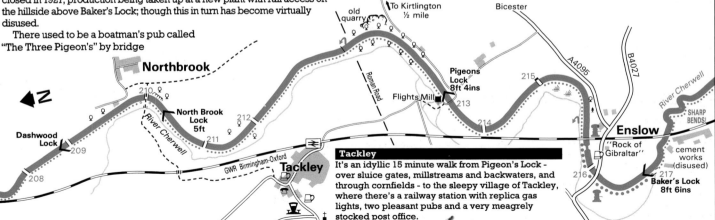

Tackley

It's an idyllic 15 minute walk from Pigeon's Lock - over sluice gates, millstreams and backwaters, and through cornfields - to the sleepy village of Tackley, where there's a railway station with replica gas lights, two pleasant pubs and a very meagrely stocked post office.

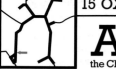

AT SHIPTON LOCK, their brief fling over, canal and river part company, though they keep affectionately in sight of one another until Thrupp, whereupon the Cherwell heads south-eastwards past Islip to become that romantic stream of The Parks, with its poets and its punts. Shipton Lock, like Aynho, is diamond shaped and not at all deep, but it can look as welcoming as a Cornish harbour in a gale when the navigable section of the Cherwell is in spate. It is a remote spot, the old lock-keeper's cottage has long been demolished. Local boaters come to picnic in the backwater of the Cherwell.

Between Shipton and Thrupp the canal widens into a shadowy lagoon fringed by beds of water lilies and reeds. The canal builders are said to have diverted a millstream here and used its bed to form the canal, a plausible explanation for an unusual yet thoroughly attractive length of waterway. Thrupp itself is almost entirely canal orientated, consisting of

little more than a drawbridge set on a tight bend, a waterway maintenance yard housed in handsome buildings of thatch and honey coloured stone, and a terrace of cottages fronting onto the canal as though it was a village street. Some of the waterway buildings predate the canal and were once part of a mill on the Cherwell. This idyllic setting figures as the location for a grisly murder in Colin Dexter's 'Inspector Morse' mystery "The Riddle of the Third Mile". The Oxford Canal in the 19th century is the setting for another book of his, "The Wench is Dead". The skies above Thrupp are filled with the drone of aircraft taking off and landing at Oxford Airport which, amongst other activities, is used as a base for training airline pilots.

Thrupp might have become a canal junction had 18th century proposals for a link between Hampton Gay and London ever got off the drawing board. The scheme was promoted in rivalry to the Grand Junction Canal and came about largely because of the poor state of the Thames at that time. In the event the Grand Junction scheme received its Royal Assent first and the London & Western Canal, as it was to be known, languished, its subscribers receiving only sixpence back in the pound on their investment.

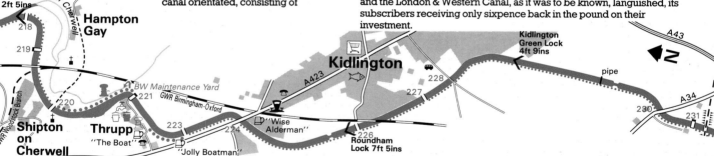

Thrupp

Two Morrells (the local Oxford brewer) pubs vie for your custom. Personally we favour THE BOAT for its unspoilt charm and excellent food, but the refurbished JOLLY BOATMAN is well worth trying too, and also offers a wide range of food.

Kidlington

Heavily suburbanised village on the northern periphery of Oxford. Useful shops, including a Co-op supermarket, Natwest, Lloyds and Midland banks ½ mile from bridges 226 & 228. Frequent buses to/from Oxford. Spar shop 3 minutes from bridge 224 where the GBG recommended WISE ALDERMAN has a canalside garden.

Wolvercote

Residential village at the top end of Port Meadow dominated by a papermill. Useful facilities easily reached from the canal at bridge 235 or the Thames at Godstow.

THE CANAL'S APPROACH to the university city of Oxford is low key and something of an anti-climax. Not for it the ethereal landscapes of the Thames and Port Meadow or the Cherwell and The Parks, but rather - with the diffidence of a freshman arriving for Michaelmas Term - it slinks in to Oxford by the tradesman's entrance, making its way modestly past the foot of gardens belonging to the Victorian houses of North Oxford's feted and erudite suburbs.

At first the countryside seems reluctant to take its cue and leave. Passing the entrance to the Duke's Cut (of which more anon) and bridged by the dual carriageway A43, the canal makes its way towards the city bordered by allotments and scattered small holdings. Residential boats, occupied by New Age travellers with nowhere to go, line its banks; or are they latter-day Scholar Gypsies, turning their backs on the Groves of Academia in favour of a sort of freedom which one finds it hard to believe can be found in the confines of a narrowboat?

Gradually the suburbs begin to make their presence felt - the playing fields of St Edwards public school; the imposing red brick homes of well-heeled dons; a factory discreetly making parts for motor cars - but these Oxford suburbs are a world away from the car plants at Cowley and the tabloid headline-grabbing estates of Blackbird Leys.

Dreamy and tree-girt the centre is sought. Lucy's Foundry is as old as the canal. Once they would cast you anything in iron you cared to mention; nowadays their order books are filled with car components. The stolid tower of St Barnabus church overlooks Oxford's two hire bases, and then an elegant iron bridge spans the entrance to Louse Lock as the Hythe Bridge arm heads for its quiet oblivion, a couple of hundred yards on.

Once upon a time the Oxford Canal terminated in a broad basin of busy wharves overlooked by the castle keep. Business was brisk in coal brought down the cut from Warwickshire, and Temple Thurston came here in search of Eynsham Harry, but in 1937 the site was acquired by William Morris, alias Lord Nuffield, for the building of a new college in his name. Since then the Oxford Canal has not so much terminated as petered out, and as the last few yards of it are occupied by residential boats, the visiting boater has no alternative but to moor back by St Barnabus and the terraced streets of Jericho, another scene of a Morse murder enquiry.

When you have drunk your fill of Oxford's wit and wisdom, and thoughts are beginning to dwell on the return journey up the cut, you might consider a detour on to the Thames, travelling upstream past Godstow and Kings locks, before rejoining the canal by way of the Duke's Cut. In most cases you will need a short stay licence for the Thames, but these are available (and relatively inexpensive) from the keeper at Osney Lock little more than five minutes walk from Hythe Bridge Street.

Armed with a Thames licence, you can drop down through Louse Lock and turn right along the Sheepwash Channel (where, sadly, the yeomen of Oxfordshire no longer gather to dip their flocks) and pass beneath the railway, noticing as you do so, the rusty remains of a railway swingbridge (with its tracks intact) which used to carry the line to the old London & North Western terminus at Rewley Road. Beyond the railway the channel emerges to join the Thames itself and you should turn right, upstream towards Godstow.

The next reach is gorgeous. Soon the tree-lined banks open out to expose the full extent of Port Meadow where cattle and horses graze against a skyline of Oxford's dreaming spires. Then the river curves round to Godstow Lock where the keeper deals in antiquarian books of Thames lore. It is worth mooring to the grassy bank upstream of Godstow's ancient stone bridge to look at the ruins of the nunnery where Henry II's mistress, Fair Rosamund, died; or, more practically, to patronise the famous "Trout Inn" overlooking the adjacent weir stream.

The Thames, known also as 'Isis' hereabouts', meanders up to Kings Lock, and though you may already be falling in love with its riverine ways, you must turn right above the lock and head back to the predictable world of the canals. The Duke's Cut was actually the original link between the canal and the river, being opened in 1789. It was owned by the Duke of Marlborough, hence the name. Boats also used it to gain access to Wolvercote paper mill, which relied on Warwickshire coal carried by canal until 1951. All too soon, passing beneath the A40 and the railway, the little Duke's Cut Lock returns you to the Oxford Canal and reality

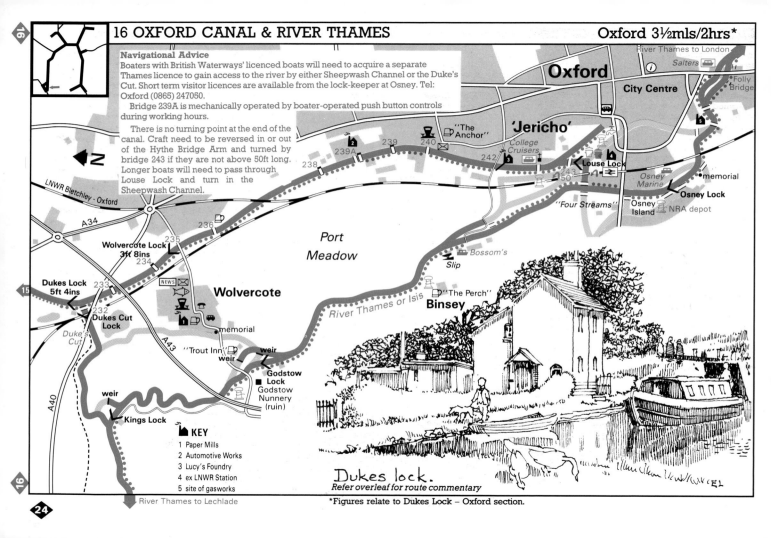

Navigational Advice

Boaters with British Waterways' licenced boats will need to acquire a separate Thames licence to gain access to the river by either Sheepwash Channel or the Duke's Cut. Short term visitor licences are available from the lock-keeper at Osney. Tel: Oxford (0865) 247050.

Bridge 239A is mechanically operated by boater-operated push button controls during working hours.

There is no turning point at the end of the canal. Craft need to be reversed in or out of the Hythe Bridge Arm and turned by bridge 243 if they are not above 50ft long. Longer boats will need to pass through Louse Lock and turn in the Sheepwash Channel.

River Thames to London

Oxford
City Centre
Salters
Folly Bridge

'Jericho'

"The Anchor"

College Cruisers

Louse Lock

Osney Marine
memorial

Osney Island

Osney Lock

NRA depot

"Four Streams"

240
239
239A
238
242
243
50

LNWR Bletchley - Oxford

N

A34

236
235

Wolvercote Lock
3ft 8ins
234

Port Meadow

Bossom's

Slip

233

Dukes Lock
5ft 4ins

NEWS

232

Dukes Cut Lock

Duke's Cut

A43

Wolvercote

memorial

"Trout Inn"
weir
weir

"The Perch"

Binsey

River Thames or Isis

A40

weir

Kings Lock

Godstow Lock
Godstow Nunnery (ruin)

KEY
1 Paper Mills
2 Automotive Works
3 Lucy's Foundry
4 ex LNWR Station
5 site of gasworks

Dukes lock.
Refer overleaf for route commentary

River Thames to Lechlade

*Figures relate to Dukes Lock – Oxford section.

Oxford reminds you of an exclusive club. The best the casual visitor can do is press their nose up against the lattice window-pane and peer enviously - or doubtless, in some cases, disdainfully - at the privileged world revealed within. Like Hardy's hero, we are all obscure Judes, in awe of this world-renowned seat of learning. Here, perhaps more than in any other English city, time stands quite literally still. Oxford makes a virtue out of tradition and nowhere else is better at transforming routine into ritual. Whole quadrangles and cloisters seem frozen into a medieval eternity where only the ubiquitous bicycles of the undergraduates break the chronological spell. From the upper deck of the open-topped tourist buses which patrol the town, the sightseer can derive a vicarious wisdom. After all, you can now truthfully recall, "When I was at Oxford!"

Eating & Drinking
THE ANCHOR - adjacent bridge 240. Comfortable suburban pub offering food.
BOOKBINDERS ARMS - rear of College Cruisers. Basic but welcoming Morrells pub, ideal for a quick pint after a thirsty day's boating.
THE TROUT - Thames-side, Godstow. Famous 12th century inn in idyllic setting overlooking a foaming weir. Equally foaming pints of Bass and a wide range of food available.
WATERMAN'S ARMS - Thames-side above Osney Lock. Cosy Morland pub offering home made food.
THE PERCH - Thames-side Binsey. Thatched riverside inn set back from the Thames behind a mask of trees. Large garden, wide menu, Wadworth on draught.
GO DUTCH - opposite railway station. Specialists in pancakes, savoury and sweet. Nice relaxing ambience.
GEORGINA'S - Covered Market. Upstairs cafe often crowded with undergraduates - don't they ever work?

Shopping
Drawing on a wide range of custom and taste - town and gown and tourists - Oxford's shops are inspired to a welcome eclecticism. The COVERED MARKET hosts the most wonderful cross-section of retailers - food, books, clothes and cafes, whilst the many branches of BLACKWELLS and a host of second-hand dealers will absorb bookworms for many a happy hour. By bridge 240, look out for BUNTERS, a charming emporium devoted to whole foods and dealing in home made Greek cooking which can be taken-away for heating up on board your boat. Telephone ahead your requirements on Oxford 57135.

Things to Do
TOURIST INFORMATION - St Aldate's, Oxford OX1 1DY. Tel: Oxford (0865) 726871.
THE OXFORD STORY - Broad Street. Tel: (0865) 728822. Open daily, admission charge. Visitors are equipped with a personal stereo providing a running commentary to displays and waxworks illustrating the history of the city and its colleges.

MUSEUM OF OXFORD - St Aldates. Tel: (0865) 815559. Open Tue-Sat.
COLLEGES - Over thirty colleges make up 'Oxford University'. Many of them are world famous such as *Balliol* and *Merton* which are both of 13th century origin; *Magdalen* (pronounced 'maudlin') which dates from 1458; and *Christ Church* founded in 1525 by Cardinal Wolsey. The general public are admitted to most of them in the afternoons.
PUNT HIRE - Oxford's traditional means of seduction can be hired from boat houses at Folly Bridge on the Thames and Magdalen Bridge on the Cherwell.
OPEN SPACES - much of Oxford's charm rests in the proliferation of green spaces, the city's lungs. These include: The Parks, Christ Church Meadow, and Port Meadow. A stroll across any of them comes as a refreshing experience after the hurly burly of the main thoroughfares, and helps to put Oxford in the context of its riverside settings.

Public Transport
BUSES - local and district services provided by the Oxford Bus Co. Tel: (0865) 711312.
TRAINS - Intercity and Network SouthEast services to/from many parts. Tel: Oxford (0865) 722333.

Boating Facilities
COLLEGE CRUISERS - Combe Road, Oxford OX2 6BL. Tel: Oxford (0865) 54343. 2 to 8 berth hire craft named after Oxford colleges, bookable direct or through Hoseasons. Pumpout, diesel, Elsan disposal, repairs & servicing, boatbuilding and fitting-out.

house lock

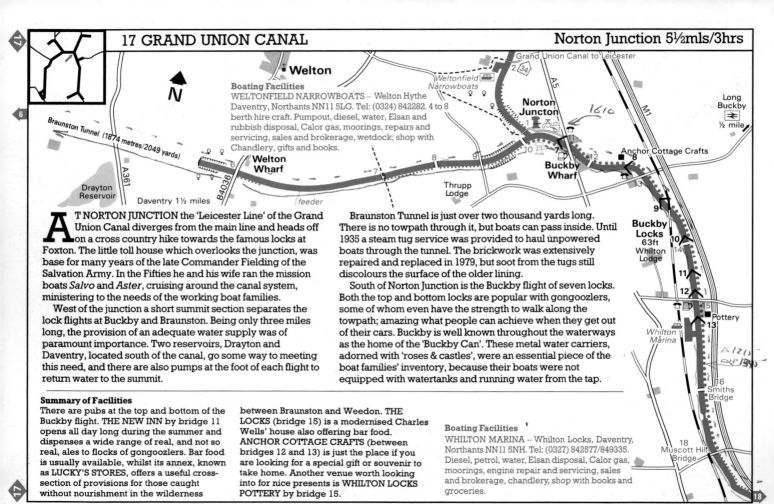

Welton

Boating Facilities
WELTONFIELD NARROWBOATS – Welton Hythe Daventry, Northants NN11 5LG. Tel: (0324) 842282. 4 to 8 berth hire craft. Pumpout, diesel, water, Elsan and rubbish disposal, Calor gas, moorings, repairs and servicing, sales and brokerage, wetdock; shop with Chandlery, gifts and books.

Grand Union Canal to Leicester

Weltonfield Narrowboats

Norton Junction

Long Buckby ½ mile

Braunston Tunnel (1874 metres/2049 yards)

Welton Wharf

Anchor Cottage Crafts

Buckby Wharf

Drayton Reservoir

Daventry 1½ miles

Thrupp Lodge

feeder

Buckby Locks 63ft Whilton Lodge

Whilton Marina

Pottery

Smiths Bridge

Muscott Hill Bridge

AT NORTON JUNCTION the 'Leicester Line' of the Grand Union Canal diverges from the main line and heads off on a cross country hike towards the famous locks at Foxton. The little toll house which overlooks the junction, was base for many years of the late Commander Fielding of the Salvation Army. In the Fifties he and his wife ran the mission boats *Salvo* and *Aster*, cruising around the canal system, ministering to the needs of the working boat families.

West of the junction a short summit section separates the lock flights at Buckby and Braunston. Being only three miles long, the provision of an adequate water supply was of paramount importance. Two reservoirs, Drayton and Daventry, located south of the canal, go some way to meeting this need, and there are also pumps at the foot of each flight to return water to the summit.

Braunston Tunnel is just over two thousand yards long. There is no towpath through it, but boats can pass inside. Until 1935 a steam tug service was provided to haul unpowered boats through the tunnel. The brickwork was extensively repaired and replaced in 1979, but soot from the tugs still discolours the surface of the older lining.

South of Norton Junction is the Buckby flight of seven locks. Both the top and bottom locks are popular with gongoozlers, some of whom even have the strength to walk along the towpath; amazing what people can achieve when they get out of their cars. Buckby is well known throughout the waterways as the home of the 'Buckby Can'. These metal water carriers, adorned with 'roses & castles', were an essential piece of the boat families' inventory, because their boats were not equipped with watertanks and running water from the tap.

Summary of Facilities

There are pubs at the top and bottom of the Buckby flight. THE NEW INN by bridge 11 opens all day long during the summer and dispenses a wide range of real, and not so real, ales to flocks of gongoozlers. Bar food is usually available, whilst its annex, known as LUCKY'S STORES, offers a useful cross-section of provisions for those caught without nourishment in the wilderness between Braunston and Weedon. THE LOCKS (bridge 15) is a modernised Charles Wells' house also offering bar food. ANCHOR COTTAGE CRAFTS (between bridges 12 and 13) is just the place if you are looking for a special gift or souvenir to take home. Another venue worth looking into for nice presents is WHILTON LOCKS POTTERY by bridge 15.

Boating Facilities
WHILTON MARINA – Whilton Locks, Daventry, Northants NN11 5NH. Tel: (0327) 842577/849335. Diesel, petrol, water, Elsan disposal, Calor gas, moorings, engine repair and servicing, sales and brokerage, chandlery, shop with books and groceries.

WHEN NAPOLEON was busy acquiring as much of Europe as he could at the beginning of the 19th century, the government got out a map of England and looked for somewhere safe to hide King George III, just in case Bonaparte actually made it across the channel. Their eye fell upon the little Northamptonshire village of Weedon which, not entirely coincidentally, had just been linked to London with the completion of William Jessop's Grand Junction Canal. Here they built barracks for two regiments and a Royal Pavilion. A canal arm led off the main line, entering the barracks through a portcullis. It was obviously intended that Weedon would be defended to the last. Napoleon, however, met his match elsewhere, and the King never actually saw his splendid pavilion. But the barracks remained in use for many years and, on occasions, troops were carried by canal boat from here to troublespots and ports of embarkation. Much of the complex remains, used inevitably now by small industrial units. Happily, though, this means that no-one seems to mind you going walkabout, imagining for yourself the military scenes of eras past.

A fifteen mile pound separates the lock flights at Buckby and Stoke Bruerne. To maintain this horizontality the canal accommodates the undulations of the Northamptonshire countryside, wrapping itself around the sinuous valley of the upper Nene; crossing the river by way of a high embankment at Weedon. The River Nene rises in lonely, upland circumstances half a dozen miles to the west, and outfalls into the Wash below the port of Wisbech; it becomes navigable at Northampton.

Weedon

Being at the junction of two trunk roads does Weedon few favours in aesthetic terms, but at least all the traffic provides good business for the village's proliferation of pubs and antique shops. If you are not anxious to meet 20th century reality full in the face, then the best part of the village is that which lies to the west of the canal. The little church is attractive too, sandwiched between the embankments of the canal and railway in a corridor of calm.

Eating & Drinking

Try the CROSSROADS HOTEL, which does excellent bar and restaurant food, THE NARROW BOAT, a Charles Wells pub on the A5 by bridge 26 at Stowe Hill, or the HEART OF ENGLAND by bridge 24 which has a wide range of real ales on offer.

Shopping

Goodness Foods have one of their health food bakeries down the road from bridge 24, but the main village shops are located to the west of the canal, and best reached from the offside moorings near the church. They include two general stores, a newsagent, butcher and post office.

Boating Facilities

CONCOFORM MARINE - The Boatyard, High Street, Weedon, Northants NN7 4QD. Tel: (0327) 40739. 2 to 10 berth hire craft in maroon, grey and black livery named (to surprisingly lyrical effect) after weeds (viz *Weed* on!) Bookable direct; members of the Blue Riband Club. Pumpout, diesel, water, Shell gas, long term moorings, maps, guides & postcards etc available from reception.
STOWE HILL MARINE (0327 41365) and WATERWAYS SERVICES (0327 42300) also offer a full range of cruising (but not hire) and boatbuilding facilities.

Nether Heyford

High House Br

29 Waterways Services
28 Standing Barn

Furnace Lane
Wharf

32

27 Flore Lane

Stowe Hill
Stowe Hill Marine

26 Stowe Hill Bridge

25 Weedon Bec

River Nene

Weedon
A5
A45

Dodford Bridge
23

24
Concoform Marine

Weedon Wharf

22 Watling Street Bridge

21 Brockhall Road Bridge

Old Barn

19 Diamond Bridge

17

18

19

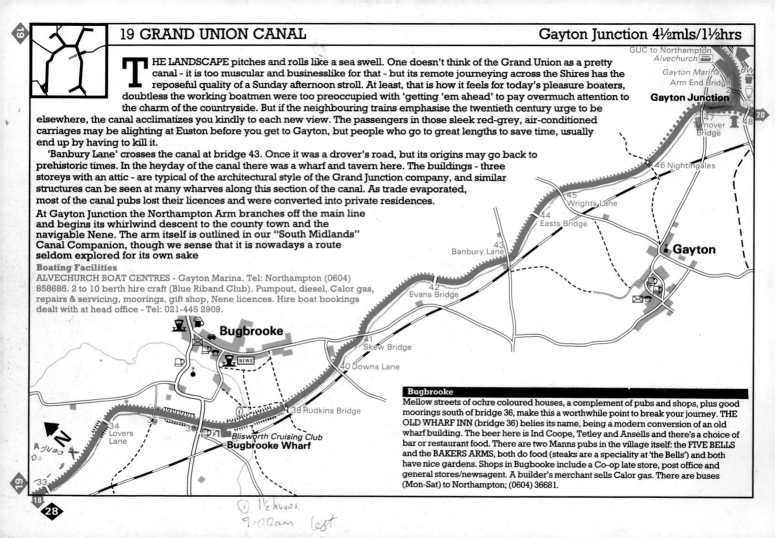

THE LANDSCAPE pitches and rolls like a sea swell. One doesn't think of the Grand Union as a pretty canal - it is too muscular and businesslike for that - but its remote journeying across the Shires has the reposeful quality of a Sunday afternoon stroll. At least, that is how it feels for today's pleasure boaters, doubtless the working boatmen were too preoccupied with 'getting 'em ahead' to pay overmuch attention to the charm of the countryside. But if the neighbouring trains emphasise the twentieth century urge to be elsewhere, the canal acclimatizes you kindly to each new view. The passengers in those sleek red-grey, air-conditioned carriages may be alighting at Euston before you get to Gayton, but people who go to great lengths to save time, usually end up by having to kill it.

'Banbury Lane' crosses the canal at bridge 43. Once it was a drover's road, but its origins may go back to prehistoric times. In the heyday of the canal there was a wharf and tavern here. The buildings - three storeys with an attic - are typical of the architectural style of the Grand Junction company, and similar structures can be seen at many wharves along this section of the canal. As trade evaporated, most of the canal pubs lost their licences and were converted into private residences.

At Gayton Junction the Northampton Arm branches off the main line and begins its whirlwind descent to the county town and the navigable Nene. The arm itself is outlined in our "South Midlands" Canal Companion, though we sense that it is nowadays a route seldom explored for its own sake

Boating Facilities
ALVECHURCH BOAT CENTRES - Gayton Marina. Tel: Northampton (0604) 858685. 2 to 10 berth hire craft (Blue Riband Club). Pumpout, diesel, Calor gas, repairs & servicing, moorings, gift shop, Nene licences. Hire boat bookings dealt with at head office - Tel: 021-445 2909.

Map labels:
GUC to Northampton
Alvechurch
Gayton Marina
Arm End Bridge
Gayton Junction
Turnover Bridge
20
48
46 Nightingales
45 Wrights Lane
44 Easts Bridge
Gayton
43 Banbury Lane
42 Evans Bridge
41 Skew Bridge
40 Downs Lane
Bugbrooke
NEWS
38 Rudkins Bridge
Blisworth Cruising Club
Bugbrooke Wharf
34 Lovers Lane
36
A 4100
N
33
18
19

Bugbrooke
Mellow streets of ochre coloured houses, a complement of pubs and shops, plus good moorings south of bridge 36, make this a worthwhile point to break your journey. THE OLD WHARF INN (bridge 36) belies its name, being a modern conversion of an old wharf building. The beer here is Ind Coope, Tetley and Ansells and there's a choice of bar or restaurant food. There are two Manns pubs in the village itself: the FIVE BELLS and the BAKERS ARMS, both do food (steaks are a speciality at 'the Bells') and both have nice gardens. Shops in Bugbooke include a Co-op late store, post office and general stores/newsagent. A builder's merchant sells Calor gas. There are buses (Mon-Sat) to Northampton; (0604) 36681.

① 1½ hours.
9:00am left

UPPER HEYFORD

SHIPTON WEIR LOCK

CROPREDY LOCK

FENNY STRATFORD

THE MARKET HARBOROUGH ARM

BLISWORTH AND STOKE BRUERNE are contrasting canalside communities separated by the longest presently navigable tunnel in Britain. It takes around half an hour to pass through; time to reflect upon the tunnel's eventful history. By the time the rest of the Grand Junction Canal had opened between London and Braunston in 1800, Blisworth still wasn't finished, despite having been under construction for seven years. A temporary tramway over the top of the hill was built in its place – traces of which are still visible – and goods laboriously transhipped from boat to wagon and back again. Finally the tunnel was opened on 25th March, 1805. A procession of boats journeyed through the tunnel from the Blisworth end. Several bands are reputed to have been aboard, and one wonders if they found the accoustics of the tunnel interior to their liking. A crowd of several thousand had assembled at the Stoke end to watch the parade of boats pass down the locks on its way to a VIP banquet at Stony Stratford.

Blisworth Tunnel's dimensions permitted narrowboats to pass inside, but no towpath was provided. At the outset boats were poled through the tunnel, rather in the manner of Oxford punts. But this practice was apparently abandoned in favour of the more traditional art of 'legging', though with, not surprisingly, a considerable number of fatalities. The canal company provided registered leggers who wore brass arm bands proclaiming their role. Later, as traffic increased, a steam tug service was provided, and although this was withdrawn as long ago as 1936, there is still a reek and an aroma of soot and steam to be savoured. In the late Seventies, in common with many other impressive canal structures, Blisworth Tunnel was feeling its age, and suffering from a backlog of indifferent maintenance. Its lining detioriated to such an extent that it became necessary to close the tunnel for four years, effectively severing the canals

of the Midlands from those of the South-east. Four million pounds was spent on re-lining the bore and the tunnel re-opened amidst much ceremony, and not a little relief amongst the boating fraternity, in August 1984.

The canal between Blisworth's southern, redbrick* portal and the top lock of the Stoke flight, bristles with boats in the summer months and steerers should handle their craft with consideration and courtesy. Keep a special eye open for the trip boats which turn in the nearby winding hole. Adjacent to the tunnel mouth are two small buildings of past significance. That nearer the tunnel was used as a bunkering and maintenance shed for the tunnel tugs. The other was a stable for the boat horses, which, of course, were led over the top of the hill to and from Blisworth. As the cutting recedes, the canal narrows through the site of Rectory Bridge, then widens as it reaches the wharf and associated buildings which, taken as a whole, make Stoke Bruerne such an attractive canal location.

A three-storey, stone built mill dominates the wharf. Now it houses the famous Museum, once it ground corn with machinery driven by a steam powered beam engine. A basin for the boats which delivered coal, stood where the grassy sward and tall poplar trees are now, and all trace has vanished of the roving bridge that carried the towpath across the entry to the dock. A row of stone cottages, originally provided for millworkers, but later used by canal employees, separates the mill from a brick house of Georgian style. For many years this was a shop catering for the needs of boat families. But in the twilight years of commercial carrying it was the home of Stoke's favourite daughter, Sister Mary Ward, a lady of high ideals and humility, who took it upon herself to look after the boat people in sickness and in health until her retirement in 1962.

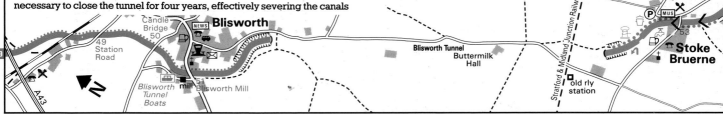

*The northern portal is of blue brick.

As trade expanded on the Grand Junction Canal, it became necessary to duplicate the locks. Here at Stoke it is interesting to discover that the top lock in use today is the duplicate chamber, the original being on the west side of the canal and used nowadays to accommodate a boat weighing machine from the Glamorganshire Canal and a BCN 'station boat', both being outdoor exhibits belonging to the museum. Buildings on the west bank of the canal include the former wharfingers office and house, now occupied by canal author, David Blagrove. Another village resident, well known in canal circles, is Brian Collings of the Guild of Waterway Artists.

Navigational Advice

No mooring is permitted in the lock flight. Free visitor moorings are provided between the tunnel mouth and the museum for a maximum of 48 hours; boats staying longer are charged. Morrings are also available at the foot of the flight - see Map 21. A 70ft winding hole is provided just south of the tunnel, and boats not proceeding south of Stoke Bruerne are advised to turn at this point. It is possible to turn a 50 foot boat above the top lock, but there is usually so much movement of trip boats etc, that to do so is to court unnecessary difficulty. Further advice on mooring and other boating matters can be obtained from the staff at the museum.

Blisworth

Church and chapel dominate the view from the canal and there are some good looking stone buildings in the village which emphasise Blisworth's former importance as a centre of quarrying. In contrast a large brick built mill dated 1879 dominates the canalside.

Eating & Drinking
ROYAL OAK - up from bridge 51. Village local offering bar food.
BLISWORTH HOTEL - west of bridge 49. Bar and restaurant meals.

Shopping
Spar grocery (with po counter) and newsagent in main street of village.

Public Transport
BUSES - United Counties to/from Northampton and Towcester. Tel: Northampton (0604) 36681.

Boating Facilities
BLISWORTH TUNNEL BOATS - Gayton Road, Blisworth, Northants NN7 3BN. Tel: (0604) 858868. 2 to 12 berth hire craft in red & cream colours named after canal tunnels. Pumpout, diesel, water, Elsan & rubbish disposal, Calor gas, moorings, repairs & servicing, boatbuilding & fitting-out, sales & brokerage. Shop with chandlery, gits and books. Dayboat hire. Outboard agents.

Stoke Bruerne

Against great odds, Stoke Bruerne transcends its popularity. In the high season it attracts the sort of ice cream crowds which any self-respecting theme park would be proud of. And yet it contrives to retain its integrity, remaining a tight-knit community with an obsessive interest in the welfare and activity of its canal. For this is a canal village without equal, and the Grand Union runs through it like a high street, so that, for once, boaters see front doors and windows, rather than back.

Eating & Drinking
THE BOAT INN has been owned by the Woodward family for over a century, a fact emphasising Stoke's sense of continuity, despite the pressures of tourism. The pub retains its identity as a 'local' too, even thought it is obviously popular with visitors. Bar meals are served and there is a range of draught beers. The landlord also operates the next door tea rooms and adjoining, first floor restaurant which has pleasant views over the expanse of water fronting the museum, even if its modern architecture strikes the only discordant note along the otherwise unspoilt waterfront. On Saturday night they host a candle-lit dinner, bookings on Roade (0604) 862428. On the opposite bank, BRUERNE'S LOCK RESTAURANT is housed in what was once a boatman's shop, bookings on Roade (0604) 863654. Stoke's newest catering establishment is the OLD CHAPEL TEA ROOM located behind the museum. Proprietors, Sally Mays and Michael Hornsby, offer the promise of "a mouthwatering selection of cakes" whilst our research crew are still raving about the ice cream.

Shopping
The popularity of the canal couldn't save Stoke from the loss of its village shop, but milk and bread are usually obtainable from the "Boat Inn" tearoom. Newspapers are available from Hillside Bungalow on the road out of the village opposite the church. When trade is brisk enough someone patrols the towpath early of a morning selling papers to overnight moorers. Two canal gift and souvenirs shops, however, do flourish, the main one being part of the museum, stocking arguably the best range of canal literature available anywhere. If you haven't a complete set of up to date editions of the "Canal Companions", then now's the time to fill the gaps!

Places to Visit
CANAL MUSEUM - canalside, Stoke Bruerne. Admission charge, open daily 10am-6pm throughout the summer, closed winter Mondays and shut at 4pm. Tel: Roade (0604) 862229. Housed in a corn mill which had closed before the Great War, the museum opened in 1963, having developed from the personal collection of the local lock-keeper, Jack James. Indoor exhibits include canal folk costumes, a boat cabin, a model of Anderton Lift which (unlike the real one) works, and many other fascinating and evocative displays. Out of doors a preserved narrowboat is usually on view. Significantly, this museum seems in no way to have suffered by the establishment of the prestigious National Waterways Museum at Gloucester, and we can recommend it wholeheartedly to boaters and other visitors alike.

NORTHAMPTONSHIRE IS A county more travelled through than visited. Lines of communication stretch across its hedged fields like strings across the frets on the neck of a guitar. Perhaps this is why these roads and railways, and this canal, appear aloof from the landscape. "Sorry can't stop," they seem to be saying: "We're just passing through." The canal traveller spends two hours negotiating the six mile pound between Stoke Bruerne and Cosgrove, and, apart from the manor house and church on the brow of the hill at Grafton, and the wharves at Yardley and Castlethorpe, it is a lonely business; a character emphasised by the stark ruins of Isworth Farm by bridge 63, the skeletal rafters of its roof inky black against the sky.

The Tove is one of those 'third division' rivers that hardly anyone outside the county has have ever heard of. Yet, by the time it joins the Great Ouse at Cosgrove, it is a significant watercourse. The Tove rises on the Uplands east of Banbury, not far from Sulgrave Manor. At the foot of Stoke Locks one arm of the river flows into the canal, being used for private moorings, whilst the other passes beneath the canal. A series of overflow weirs are bridged by the towpath. South of Bozenham Mill the river forms the boundary with Buckinghamshire.

Stoke Locks form another step in the Grand Union's roller-coaster ride between London and Birmingham: the old Grand Junction Canal had summits at Tring and Braunston, and when the route was amalgamated with the Warwick & Birmingham Canal in 1929 a third summit was added at Olton, near Solihull. Most visitors to Stoke Bruerne – if they bother to stretch their legs at all – walk from the top lock towards the tunnel. But the rest of the flight has plenty of interest, not least the obvious remains of the short-lived duplicate locks and the disused side ponds. There is a pump house at the foot of the flight for returning water to the upper pound.

BAXTER BOATFITTING SERVICES – The Wharf, Yardley Gobion, Northants NN12 7UE. Tel: Milton Keynes (0908) 542844. Pumpout, diesel, Calor gas, solid fuel, drydock, slipway, boatfitting, repairs & servicing (including emergency call-outs), surveys and restorations.

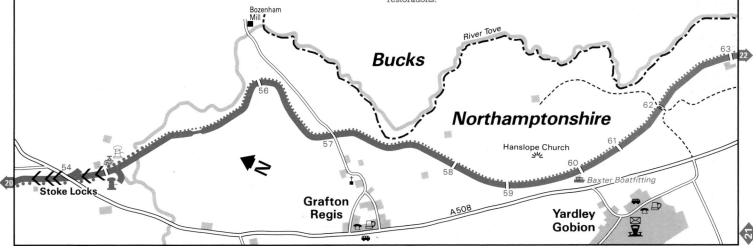

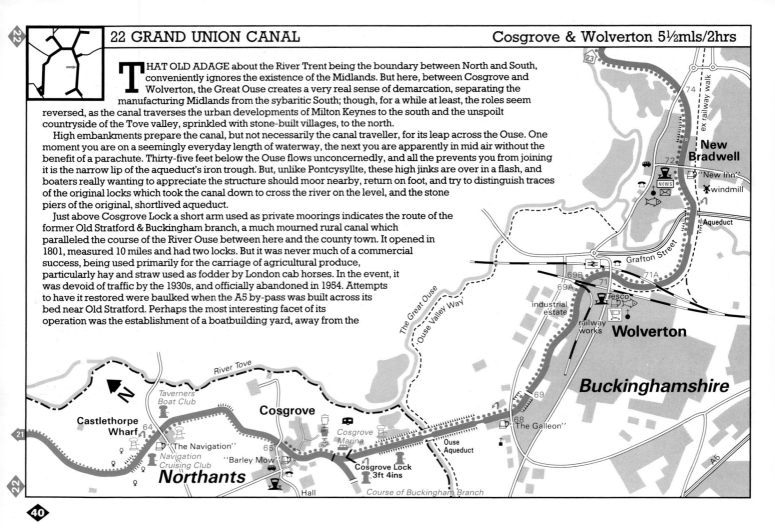

THAT OLD ADAGE about the River Trent being the boundary between North and South, conveniently ignores the existence of the Midlands. But here, between Cosgrove and Wolverton, the Great Ouse creates a very real sense of demarcation, separating the manufacturing Midlands from the sybaritic South; though, for a while at least, the roles seem reversed, as the canal traverses the urban developments of Milton Keynes to the south and the unspoilt countryside of the Tove valley, sprinkled with stone-built villages, to the north.

High embankments prepare the canal, but not necessarily the canal traveller, for its leap across the Ouse. One moment you are on a seemingly everyday length of waterway, the next you are apparently in mid air without the benefit of a parachute. Thirty-five feet below the Ouse flows unconcernedly, and all the prevents you from joining it is the narrow lip of the aqueduct's iron trough. But, unlike Pontcysyllte, these high jinks are over in a flash, and boaters really wanting to appreciate the structure should moor nearby, return on foot, and try to distinguish traces of the original locks which took the canal down to cross the river on the level, and the stone piers of the original, shortlived aqueduct.

Just above Cosgrove Lock a short arm used as private moorings indicates the route of the former Old Stratford & Buckingham branch, a much mourned rural canal which paralleled the course of the River Ouse between here and the county town. It opened in 1801, measured 10 miles and had two locks. But it was never much of a commercial success, being used primarily for the carriage of agricultural produce, particularly hay and straw used as fodder by London cab horses. In the event, it was devoid of traffic by the 1930s, and officially abandoned in 1954. Attempts to have it restored were baulked when the A5 by-pass was built across its bed near Old Stratford. Perhaps the most interesting facet of its operation was the establishment of a boatbuilding yard, away from the canal itself, at Stony Stratford specialising in the construction of small sea-going vessels, which had to be hauled by traction engine along the Watling Street and launched into the canal for transfer to London.

If you were abandoned blindfolded on the towpath of the Grand Union as it winds through Wolverton, your first glimpse after struggling free of your bonds would suggest that you had been dumped on the BCN. High brick factory walls frame the canal and a tall chimney dominates it. This is no Black Country foundry, but rather what's left of the celebrated workshops of the London & North Western Railway, renowned for the building of carriages and wagons to the highest standards. Sadly the railway's own fire station has been demolished to make way for a supermarket, but another aspect of the company's welfare, a sports ground and stadium, can be seen by bridge 71.

The canal takes to an embankment as it skirts the industrial village of New Bradwell. In working boat days the boat women would hobble down the hill in their voluminous skirts to shop, catching up with their unstopping boats at the other end of the embankment. They would not recognise the huge new aqueduct carrying the canal over Grafton Street. Will its designers, Pell Frischmann, join Telford and Rennie in the pantheon of bridge builders? We think not. Up on the hillside the sales of a restored windmill peep over the treetops, down in the valley of the Ouse flooded-out sandpits have created attractive expanses of water.

Cosgrove

A quiet village away from the main road with some attractive stone buildings. On the off-side a fine row of poplar trees frames the parkland of the hall. An unusual pedestrian tunnel (once used by boat horses to reach the pub stables) passes beneath the canal, whilst bridge 65 is unusually ornate. Sand was worked commercially down the confluence of the Tove and Ouse. A narrow gauge railway linked the sand pits with the canal wharf and some of the rails remain in situ by the old canal junction.

Eating & Drinking

THE NAVIGATION - adjacent bridge 64. Splendid free house with imaginative cycle of independent brews on draught. Home made food, garden, families catered for.

BARLEY MOW - canalside, Cosgrove village. Refurbished stone-built pub offering meals from their 'Country Kitchen' both sessions. Children welcome if eating, skittles, garden with limited customer moorings (but also access from opposite towpath side via tunnel). Interesting canal archive photographs adorn the walls.

Ouse Aqueduct.

Shopping

Post office stores open daily except Sunday, half day on Thursday.

Boating Facilities

COSGROVE MARINA - lockside. Tel: Milton Keynes (0908) 562467. Moorings, boatbuilding, fitting-out, repairs & servicing.

LINDA CRUISES - public and charter boat trips. Tel: MK 563377.

Wolverton

A manufacturing town seemingly cast adrift from its Midlands moorings and washed aground in rural Buckinghamshire. Lots of workaday pubs, Indian and Italian restaurants and fish & chip shops. Large new Tesco store accessible from bridge 71 plus local shops, Lloyds and Barclays banks. Frequent Network SouthEast trains from the canalside station.

New Bradwell

A community of terraced streets built as homes for the employees of Wolverton railway works. Useful shops adjacent to bridge 72 and a nice pub, the NEW INN, Adnams, Charles Wells, bar & restaurant meals, families welcome, garden.

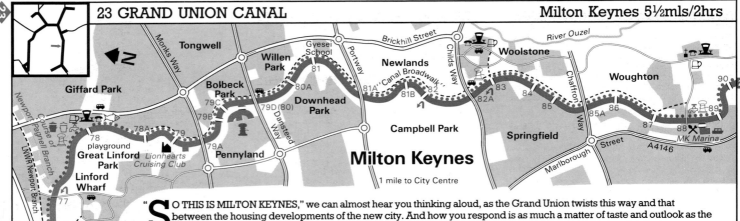

"**S**O THIS IS MILTON KEYNES,**"** we can almost hear you thinking aloud, as the Grand Union twists this way and that between the housing developments of the new city. And how you respond is as much a matter of taste and outlook as the car you drive and the coffee you drink. Personally, we found it fascinating. The variety of architectural styles is as diverse as it is eclectic. One welcomes the good honest use of brick and timber, the refusal to be hidebound and categorised, the informality, the heterogeneity, the vernacular splashes of weatherboarding and pantiles; the canal's role as a linear park. But what surprised us was the sheer un-Englishness of it all. Communal drives, patios and lawns seem at odds with Anglo Saxon reserve. Is Milton Keynes a hot house for a new generation of gregarious Britons?

But, inevitably, there are disappointments. One would have liked to have seen more integration of houses and water; more examples of the admirable Pennyland Basin where arms off the canal have been allowed to penetrate in and around individual dwellings, so that those inhabitants with boats can 'park' them in aquatic driveways. And the other drawback is the lack of formal visitor moorings conveniently placed for access to the city centre. Boaters need moorings in urban environments just as much as motorists need car parks, and would correspondingly be happy to pay appropriately for such facilities. A rank of secure and attractive 'fishbone' jetties by Child's Way would encourage far more waterborne visitors to seek out the centre. Our research crew ploughed on and on through the suburbs and missed the centre completely – and they are *paid* to look out for such things.

Amidst all these Brave New World developments, it is easy to forget that the canal predates the city by a century and a half or more. Old maps show the canal traversing a rolling landscape of scattered hamlets and the working boatmen of the past would surely be astonished at the transformation. The only canalside settlements of any note along this section were at Great Linford and Woughton on the Green. The former was notable as the point from which a branch canal led to Newport Pagnell. It had been opened in 1817 but was closed by 1846, much of its course being taken over by the branch railway, itself now converted into a pleasant public footpath. An interpretive board by bridge 77 indicates the course of the Newport Pagnell Canal and recommends a short detour from the towpath to trace its remains. The railway closed in 1964 and was steam worked by push & pull to the end.

KEY
old brick kilns

Great Linford

Magically idyllic manorial village, sympathetically encapsulated within the new city's development zone. Moor up and stroll along its neatly gravelled paths; listen to the birdsong; watch the pond life; admire the church, manor and almshouses. Pub, shop and frequent weekday bus service to Milton Keynes. THE BLACK HORSE INN – canalside bridge 76 – is a popular and comfortable three centuries old pub with a nice waterside garden, bar and restaurant food.

Giffard Park

A new housing development of chief interest to canal users for its facilities. The GIFFARD PARK is a modern Whitbread 'Brewer's Fayre' establishment usually open all day and offering a variety of meals; it also includes a family lounge, small garden and excellent customer moorings. Across the road stand post office stores, a Chinese fish & chip shop and an off licence. Buses leave at frequent intervals for the city centre.

Woolstone

The original village has all but been engulfed by new housing, but THE BARGE (a Toby Inns grill) and the post office stores lie handily close to bridge 83, and there is a reasonably frequent bus service into the city.

Milton Keynes

The truth is, of course, that Milton Keynes is not in England at all, neither does it belong to the same time zone most of us inhabit; if you want a comparison, try Los Angeles in the year 2005. Whether or not the planners had this in mind when work began on the new city in 1967, is open to conjecture, but by the turn of the century the population will have risen to 200,000 and you can't fool all of the people all of the time. Riding its boulevards in the shuttle buses, walking through the steel and glass malls of its shopping centre, where giant palms cast shadows on terazzio tiles, one is left floundering for a response; as ambivalent of its pros and cons as a critic at the first night of an avant garde production.

Eating & Drinking
THE MOORINGS – canalside bridge 88.

Shopping
"Europe's finest shopping experience," to quote the publicity blurb. The main shopping area lies between Midsummer and Silbury Boulevards, about 1½ miles west of the canal. The cast list is certainly impressive, and it would be difficult to think of a retail chain not represented here. Grocery markets are held on Tuesdays and Saturdays and a craft market on Thursdays. Refreshments are available from a variety of establishments: wine bars, Italian restaurants, store cafes and a branch of McDonalds.

Things to Do
TOURIST INFORMATION CENTRE – Saxon Court, Avebury Boulevard, Milton Keynes MK9 3HS. Tel: Milton Keynes (0908) 692692.
Attractions in MK tend to be resident rather than visitor based. But if you have the time, then the famous Peace Pagoda off Brickhill Street (near bridge 81) is certainly very moving. The TIC also stocks numerous descriptive leaflets on local walks, many of which incorporate sections of the towpath.

Public Transport
BUSES – an excellent network of 'Street Shuttles' provides easy access to/from the city centre. Tel: MK (0908) 668366.
TRAINS – InterCity and Network SouthEast services from the central station. Tel: MK (0908) 370883.

Boating Facilities
MILTON KEYNES MARINA – Waterside, Peartree Bridge, Milton Keynes MK6 3BX. Tel: MK (0908) 672672. Comprehensive facilities, chandlery, moorings etc.

Moorings
We have already recorded our disappointment at the lack of formal moorings close to the city centre. Perhaps in due course someone will take note. In the meantime the best policy for boaters wishing to visit central Milton Keynes is to tie up at one of the peripheral villages and catch a bus into the centre. Great Linford, Giffard Park, Woolstone and Simpson are ideal for this. Alternatively, excellent visitor moorings are also provided by Milton Keynes Marina (bridge 88).

FENNY STRATFORD LOCK marks the commencement of the Grand Union's climb out of the valley of the Ouse up towards the Chilterns and the summit at Tring. But, with a rise of a meagre foot, its contribution to the ascent is not impressive. In fact, it was not planned in the original survey, being built as a supposedly temporary measure to alleviate excess water pressures experienced on the long pound between here and Cosgrove. Tradition has it that southbound working boats in a hurry used to burst their way through whichever gates happened to be shut at the time, a habit the authorities would doubtless respond to with court summonses today. In any case, the lock comes as welcome exercise after the three or four hours spent glued to the tiller if you have come straight down from Cosgrove. And the environment provides a happy assembly, being comprised of several canalside cottages, an old boatman's pub, a swing bridge capable of spanning the chamber, and the most northerly of

the 'Northern Engine' pump houses, open as a cafe and craft shop during the summer months.

'Finney' marks the southern extent of Milton Keynes' sprawl, though it is hardly characteristic of it, being a much older town. Travelling southwards it is, in many ways, reassuring to be back in the familiar world of semi-detached suburbs. Fenny Wharf was a busy spot on the canal; coal was brought to the gas works and flour and sugar carried from London Docks for Valentine's mill. The Grand Junction Company's own warehouse still stands by bridge 96. As the canal emerges from its urban environment there are pleasant views across the River Ouzel and Watling Street towards the elevated heathlands of Woburn and Aspley.

Northwards from Fenny Stratford the Grand Union is bordered briefly by factories before skirting the old village of Simpson on an embankment. A small aqueduct, invisible from the canal, accommodates a footpath. There are glimpses to the east of Walton Hall, headquarters of the Open University.

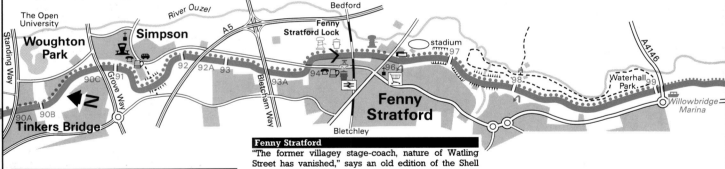

Simpson

Another of Milton Keynes's antecedent villages. Facilities include a post office stores selling newspapers, buses to the city centre, and a public phone. (Which reminds us, the further south you go, the more likely telephones are to be card, rather than coin, operated!) THE PLOUGH is a very pleasant Charles Wells pub with a garden backing onto the canal. Bar and restaurant meals are usually available.

Fenny Stratford

"The former villagey stage-coach, nature of Watling Street has vanished," says an old edition of the Shell Guide to Buckinghamshire, and that sadly sums up Fenny Stratford's slightly impoverished air. The adjoining new town of Bletchley is the local hub of activity now, leaving Fenny in the role of a suburb. Nevertheless it is an amenable place to moor and there are useful shops a short distance from bridge 96. Likewise, there are several pubs, the RED LION being canalside by the lock; a hospitable, but basic local with no pretensions to the tourist trade.

Boating Facilities

WILLOWBRIDGE ENTERPRISES – Stoke Road, Bletchley. MK2 3JZ Tel: Milton Keynes (0908) 643242. Pumpout, diesel, petrol, Calor gas, Elsan & rubbish disposal, moorings, repairs & servicing, fitting-out, DIY facilities, boat lift, sales & brokerage, slipway, showers and laundry, chandlery, provisions, off-licence, gifts & payphone

THE GRAND UNION has probably appeared more often in the annals of canal literature than any other canal. Classics, both fictional and factual, such as "The Water Gipsies", "Maiden's Trip", "Hold on a Minute" and "Bread Upon the Waters" successfully capture its atmosphere as a working waterway, but don't really prepare you for its beauty as it unravels through the Ouzel valley, past the sandy, bracken covered hills of Linslade and over the border from Bucks to Beds. The Ouzel seems to shift some of its riverine quality upon the canal; as in all good friendships, there is a degree of exchange in character. Between bridges 109 and 111 the 'Cross Bucks Way' offers towpath walkers a pretty detour above the canal past the isolated church and manor house at Old Linslade.

The Ouzel rises on the Dunstable Downs, and flows northwards to join the Great Ouse at Newport Pagnell. It used to be a river of watermills. Here and there these survive as private dwellings, unhappily no longer fulfilling their original function; though who knows, in our environmentally conscious age windmills and watermills may come back into their own once again. Paper Mill was listed in the Domesday Survey. Leighton Mill did, however, develop industrially and has become part of the Rank Hovis empire. Its premises can be seen across the river opposite the attractive boatyard of Wyvern Shipping.

Soulbury Locks – known to working boatmen as the 'Stoke Hammond Three' – have a total rise of 20 feet. Overlooked by a popular pub and provided with a picnic site, they are the ultimate gongoozlers flight, and if any of your crew suffer from stage fright this is not the best of places for them to freeze when operating the locks. The old engine house here is now occupied by an ironwork workshop, and features displays of bygones and crafts which visitors are welcome to look around.

The three mile pound between Soulbury and Leighton locks is captivating. Beyond the watermeadows of the Ouzel mixed woodland clothes a ridge of heathland. Looping around Old Linslade, the canal encounters "The Globe", a pretty, weatherboarded inn which possibly predates the Grand Junction.

Eating & Drinking
Two well known canalside pubs tempt you to pause along this length of the canal. At Soulbury Locks the eponymous THREE LOCKS does a roaring trade with motorists fascinated by the activity of the locks. A wide range of food is usually available at this Aylesbury Brewery Company house. Of equal popularity, THE GLOBE, by bridge 111 is a much older building, predating the canal, attractively weatherboarded and offering Marstons and Ruddles on draught together with a good choice of food and a large garden with childrens play area.

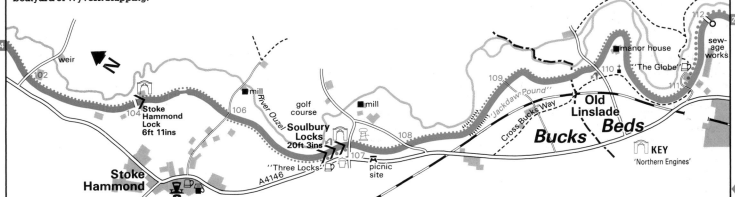

INTERRUPTED BRIEFLY, but not overwhelmed, by the shared urban environments of Linslade and Leighton Buzzard, the Grand Union continues its predominantly rural progress, crossing the boundary between the counties of Bedford and Buckingham, and sprinkled with solitary locks at regular intervals. Each lock has its own atmosphere and ambience. Leighton Lock is overlooked by a substantial, whitewashed lock-keeper's house; by Grove Lock there is a stone milepost advertising the distance to the Thames; and adjacent to Church Lock what was once the smallest chapel in Buckinghamshire has been converted into a private residence.

In the early years of the Grand Junction water shortages were experienced and, to go some way to alleviate the problem, a sequence of narrowbeam chambers were duplicated alongside the original wide locks. These allowed single boats to use less water and also enabled the canal to cope better with its growing traffic. Remains of these locks are apparent at several locations and explain the provision of extra arches on a number of bridges. A series of pumping engines were also introduced to return water to the summit. Most of the characteristic engine houses remain. By and large they are gaunt and ghostly structures now, redolent of a time when the canal was in business to make a profit for its shareholders; though one or two have been adapted for new use. Working boatmen called them the 'Northern Engines', and naturally there were regular deliveries of coal by boat to stoke the boilers.

Leighton Buzzard is a centre of the sand industry. Well into the era of the Beatles and the Stones narrowboats were still involved in the carriage of this commodity and there is plenty of evidence of former wharves. A network of narrow gauge railways connected such loading points with the sand pits themselves.

Street, stockists of sports equipment now but still advertising their origins as saddle and harness makers. Also of note: the excellent outdoor clothing shop at the foot of the High Street, the proliferation of wine merchants and JACKSONS the bakers from Aylesbury.

Leighton Buzzard

An unexpectedly delightful town with a refreshing period feel; especially on Tuesdays when the handsome High Street is covered in market stalls. A wealth of good architecture spans the centuries – the perfect antidote to the high-tech of Milton Keynes. Arguably the most interesting town on the whole of the old Grand Junction.

Eating & Drinking

LA BUSE – charming and inexpensive French restaurant on High Street by the bus stops.

SWAN HOTEL – High Street. Egon Ronay recommended former coaching inn. Restaurant meals in the conservatory; lunch around £12, dinner £20.
Pubs worth trying include: RED LION (Ind Coope) North St; BLACK LION (Benskins Heritage Inn) High St; and THE GOLDEN BELL adjacent to the post office.

Shopping

Contrasting styles in the traditional High Street and neighbouring Bossard precinct, but lots of nice individual retailers continue to flourish, like LINNEY & SON on Lake

Boating Facilities

THE WYVERN SHIPPING CO LTD – Rothschild Road, Linslade, Leighton Buzzard, Beds LU7 7TF. Tel: LB (0525) 372355. 2 to 8 berth hire craft in red & blue livery bookable through Blakes or direct. Pumpout, diesel, water, gas short term moorings, repairs & servicing, boatbuilding & fitting-out, drydock. Long established hire base dating back to 1954.
LEIGHTON LADY CANAL CRUISES – 2 Canalside, Leighton Buzzard. Tel: LB (0525) 384563. Public and private charter trips.

SAND GIVES WAY to clay, and clay to chalk, as the canal begins to take seriously the need to climb up to the Chilterns. Locks occur more frequently and there is little point in those responsible for working them to reboard the boat in the intervening pounds. In any case it's fun to tramp the towpath for a change, gazing eastwards to the furzy escarpment of the Dunstable Downs where, on a clear day, you can make out the chalk lion of Whipsnade and watch gliders making the most of the thermals above the rounded rampart of Ivinghoe Beacon. A mile and a half's walk from bridge 123 will take you to the National Trust's Pitstone Windmill.

A sense of remoteness seems to settle on the countryside. The boat people knew this stretch of canal as 'the fields', a typically simple but eloquent description. The isolation is underlined when you recall that the Great Train Robbery took place on the lonely section of line north of Cheddington station in 1963. The Grand Junction was a canal obsessed with time. Everything was date-stamped: lock-chambers, bridges, tie-bars, mooring rings, paddle gear. You are tempted to indulge in a sort of Victorian parlour game in which you must attach an important event to each date you come across.

Cheddington

This straggling commuter village, noted for fruit growing, can be reached by road from Horton and Cooks wharves, or by lane and path from Ivinghoe Locks. It has three pubs, two of them - the ROSEBERY ARMS near the station, and the OLD SWAN, a quaint, thatched affair at the southern end of the village - well worth patronising. There is also a post office and a good general store (open Sun am). The isolated station (from which there are views of Mentmore, once the country seat of the Rothschilds) is served by local trains between Milton Keynes and Euston, and forms a useful staging post between Leighton Buzzard and Tring for the benefit of towpath walkers.

Pistone Green

A workaday village dominated by Castle Cement's huge factory. It boasts a pub and general store, but thirsty, hungry canallers need go no further than the DUKE OF WELLINGTON adjacent to bridge 126, an excellent Morland pub offering a good range of food.

Boating Facilities

GREBE CANAL CRUISES - Pitstone Wharf, Leighton Buzzard, Beds LU7 9AD. Tel: Aylesbury (0296) 661920. 4 to 6 berth hire craft in red & blue named after varieties of birds. Electric trip boat and day boat hire. Pumpout, diesel, water, Elsan & rubbish disposal, Calor gas, long term moorings, repairs & servicing, sales & brokerage, slipway, DIY facilities and gift shop.

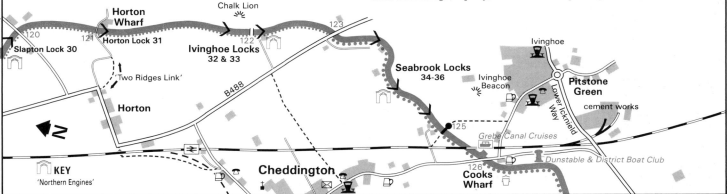

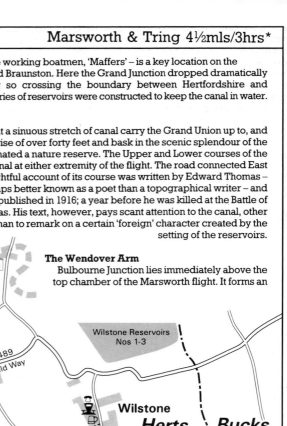

MARSWORTH – or, in the *patois* of the working boatmen, 'Maffers' – is a key location on the canal's journey between London and Braunston. Here the Grand Junction dropped dramatically from its Tring summit – in doing so crossing the boundary between Hertfordshire and Buckinghamshire – and, as traffic grew, a series of reservoirs were constructed to keep the canal in water.

Marsworth Locks

Seven closely grouped chambers set about a sinuous stretch of canal carry the Grand Union up to, and down from, the summit. They have a total rise of over forty feet and bask in the scenic splendour of the adjoining reservoirs; themselves designated a nature reserve. The Upper and Lower courses of the prehistoric Icknield Way cross the canal at either extremity of the flight. The road connected East Anglia with Salisbury Plain. A delightful account of its course was written by Edward Thomas – perhaps better known as a poet than a topographical writer – and published in 1916; a year before he was killed at the Battle of Arras. His text, however, pays scant attention to the canal, other than to remark on a certain 'foreign' character created by the setting of the reservoirs.

The Wendover Arm

Bulbourne Junction lies immediately above the top chamber of the Marsworth flight. It forms an

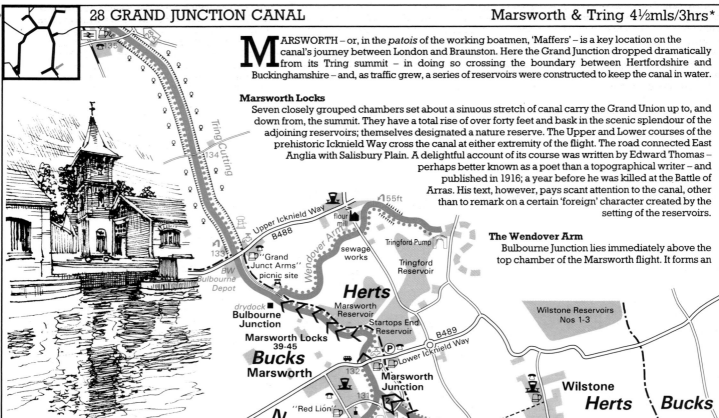

Reflections at Bulbourne.

Figures refer to Main Line lock 37 to Cowroast. Allow 2½hrs for this section of the Aylesbury Arm.

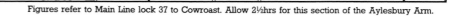

attractive canalscape; a covered drydock and a junction house providing particularly graceful features. Here a welcome supply of water enters the main line from the Wendover Arm, a branch built primarily with this role in mind; though a flour mill and the famous boatbuilding yard of Bushell Bros. brought extra activity. The arm's course originally extended to just over six miles, but it was prone to seepage and a central section was abandoned in 1904. Nowadays it can be navigated up to the 55 foot maximum winding hole beyond Heygates bustling flour mill, providing boaters with a whimsical little detour of considerable charm. The towpath is extant throughout and, with railway stations at both Wendover and Tring, is a popular excursion for Londoners.

Tring Cutting

Just south of Bulbourne Junction stand the elegant canal workshops of the same name. The principal activity here is the manufacture of lock gates and you may well glimpse some of the vast timbers involved in the process lying in or around the yard. Beyond the depot the canal passes beneath the Upper Icknield Way and enters Tring Cutting. Stretching for 1½ miles and reaching a maximum depth of 30 feet, the cutting is said to have taken the best part of five years to dig. With equipment no more sophisticated than pick-axes and wheel-barrows this is not a surprising statistic. But the labour of two centuries ago seems nebulous now. Nature long ago reclaimed the gash in her side, soothed it with vegetation, and created a chasm of narcotic splendour. For an absolute contrast, take the lane which crosses turnover bridge 134 to view the parallel railway cutting engineered by Robert Stephenson, an altogether more ambitious affair - as befits its time - and one still penetrated by the frequent passage of trains upon its four tracks.

Marsworth

A quiet, unassuming village on the border of Bucks and Herts. Nice church with flint tower overlooking the canal.

Eating & Drinking

THE RED LION - adjacent bridge 130. A classic village pub with a wonderfully uncontrived timeless atmosphere. Easily one of the best pubs we have encountered anywhere on the canal system. Beers include Wadworth, Banks & Taylor and Hook Norton. Lunchtime and evening food daily but for Sundays. Bar billiards, nice little garden. Two 'runners-up' in the WHITE LION and ANGLER'S RETREAT by bridge 132.

Shopping

THE SHIP - canalside bridge 130. In the canal's heyday this delightful thatched canalside dwelling was a boatman's pub. For many years now, however, it has been licenced as a shop dealing in groceries, newspapers, beers, wines and canal souvenirs. There is also a shop in the village centre.

Public Transport

BUSES - regular Aylesbury-Dunstable service. Tel: Aylesbury (0296) 84919.

Bulbourne

No shops, but the GRAND JUNCTION ARMS by bridge 133 is a justly popular pub offering Benskins beers and food (to eat in or take-away) both sessions; its large canalside garden overlooks the waterway workshops.

Wilstone

Small village by the Aylesbury Arm. Lovely little pub called the HALF MOON, village store and solid fuel merchant.

Aylesbury

In spite of its status as the county town of Buckinghamshire, Aylesbury is a comparitively small place. It became an administrative centre when Buckingham was partially destroyed by fire in 1725. One's first impressions are tainted by a surfeit of glass, and concrete and traffic. But the old heart of the town, centred on the market place with its statues, cobbles, clocktower and handsome municipal buildings, is on a reassuringly human scale. Deeper into the town, along attractive lanes and alleyways, you come upon the substantial parish church of St Mary's; the highest, and probably most peaceful point in Aylesbury.

Eating & Drinking

THE SHIP - cosy little street corner pub backing onto the basin. Benskins, Tetley and Guinness on draught, bar lunches Mon-Sat.
WHITE SWAN - Walton Street (opposite bus station). Good food and locally brewed Chiltern Beechwood bitter.
THE ARISTOCRAT - Wendover Road (turn left out of basin - 3 mins walk). Fullers ales and bar food.

Shopping

The town centre is less than 5 minutes from the canal basin. Two precincts house most of the retail chains. The High Street is pedestrianised and W.H. Smiths and McDonalds can be found on it. Jacksons the bakers seem to pop up everywhere, but canal folk don't have to go far because the bakery backs onto the basin: nice cream cakes for those who've just lock-wheeled down from Marsworth.

Public Transport

BUSES - Luton & District. Tel: Aylesbury (0296) 84919.
TRAINS - services to/from London Marylebone. Tel: High Wycombe (0494) 441561.

THE THREE MILE Tring Summit section stretches between Bulbourne and Cowroast. As the canal emerges from Tring Cutting there are views above the beechwoods east to the urn-topped column which stands on Albury Common, about a mile and a half east of Tring railway station. The monument was erected in 1832 in the memory of the doyen of canal promoters, Francis Egerton, the third Duke of Bridgewater. The neighbouring estate of Ashridge House was one of the 'Canal Duke's' properties, albeit one that he allowed to fall into ruin. Inside the column a staircase climbs to a viewing balcony 200 feet above the ground, and it is open to the public under the aegis of the National Trust on summer weekends.

In contrast to the graceful splendour of the Duke's monument and its sylvan setting, the opposite bank of the canal is occupied by a 'Buffer Depot', a semi-secret government establishment used for the storage of supplies held pending a national emergency. This one abuts a well-piled wharf, suggesting that the Civil Service has more faith in the Grand Union's capacity for commercial trade than British Waterways. Cowroast is a popular boating centre, a large lagoon providing moorings for private craft off the main line. The lock here is picturesque and well cared for. Look out for the pump house, the cast-iron span of bridge 137 and the former 'control' office which correlated boat movements up and down the Grand Union in carrying days.

South of Cowroast the 'Grand Junction' commences its journey down to the Thames at Brentford. All of a sudden the canal and neighbouring landscape comes under the thrall of the capital and there are 'Green Line' bus stops along the A41 which enable the people around you to be in Piccadilly faster

than you can get to Berkhamstead. A steady procession of locks takes the canal along the valley of the little River Bulbourne: a fine old mill converted into flats separates the two locks at Dudswell; Northchurch Locks were known as 'Gas Two' because they used to be overlooked by Berkhamstead Gas works, but now the site is occupied by industrial units. Tennis courts, recreation grounds and a little non-league football stadium herald the approach to Berkhamstead, a town which takes a pride in the appearance of its canal and, by the same token, creates a favourable impression with canal travellers, be they on foot or afloat. Graffiti and vandalism are conspicuously absent as the canal moves agreeably along its corridor between the railway and the A41. A totem pole in a canalside timber yard and a well cared for boatyard add interest and incident to the journey and the canal has been

Berkhamsted

Castle

Town Centre

Berkhamsted Locks
16ft 10ins

Northchurch Locks
27ft

Northchurch

Bridgewater Boats

Northchurch Common

B4506

Dudswell

Dudswell Locks
13ft 4ins Nos. 47 & 48

R. Bulbourne

A41

Bridgewater Monument

Cowroast Marina

Cowroast Lock

Cowroast

Buffer Depot

54 55
142
141
53
52
51
140
50
139
49
48
47
46 6ft
137
136

N

cleansed of "that odd gritty smell blowing up from the coal barges" which Graham Greene, whose father was headmaster at the nearby school, recalled. Nothing in the character of the canal suggests it, but south of here, all the way to Brentford and the tidal Thames, the Grand Union is (or should that be was?) officially regarded as a widebeam waterway; but that, as they say, is another story.

Berkhamstead

'Berko' (in working boatman's parlance) is a nice little town inhabited by nice Home Counties types who look as though they've just stepped out of an episode of "Mrs Dale's Diary". The A41 constitutes the main thoroughfare; a road, which in its travels from London to Birkenhead, encounters more canals than most. The town's best buildings are its oldest: the flint built parish church of St Peter and the ruined Norman castle, once the residence of the Black Prince.

Eating & Drinking

Two canalside pubs of contrasting character deserve your custom. THE BOAT (canalside bridge 142) is a comfortable, modernised Fuller's pub offering excellent food along with the Chiswick brewery's prize-winning ales, whilst with its frontage attractively overlooking lock 55 is THE RISING SUN, an altogether more down to earth Benskins pub which looks as though the last of its working boatman patrons has just left with a cargo for Limehouse. In Castle Street (reached via bridge 141)

the CASTLE TEA ROOM is delightfully genteel and offers (in addition to atmosphere) coffees, light lunches and cream teas.

Shopping

Berkhamstead's little shops are full of character and include a first class fishmongers and some equally fine butchers. All the big four banks have branches along the A41 and there are supermarkets if you must have them. As an antidote, explore the old Town Hall arcade of craft and health food shops; one of the outlets concentrates exclusively on teddy bears - you have been warned!

Public Transport

TRAINS - frequent Network SouthEast local trains to/from London Euston and Milton Keynes, calling at Tring, Cheddington and Leighton Buzzard to the benefit of towpath walkers.

Boating Facilities

BRIDGEWATER BOATS - Castle Wharf, Berkhamsted, Hertfordshire Tel: (0442) 863615 2 to 8

berth hire craft in red & white named, very fetchingly, after characters in T.S. Eliot's "Possum Book of Cats". Pumpout, diesel, water, Calor gas, repairs & servicing, sales & brokerage, slipway, long term moorings at Cassio Bridge, Watford. Interior design service for boatbuilders.

Cowroast

Nothing to do with bovine barbecues, but a corruption of 'cow rest', a throwback to cattle droving days. The big, eponymous roadside inn predates the canal. It does bar and restaurant meals and offers Benskins (former Watford brewer - beer now comes from Ind Coope's huge plant at Burton-on-Trent) beers.

Boating Facilities

COWROAST/MIDLAND CHANDLERS - Cowroast Marina, Tring, Herts HP23 5RE. Tel: (0442) 823222. Pumpout, diesel, water, Elsan and refuse disposal, Calor gas, moorings, repairs & servicing, sales & brokerage, drydock, DIY facilities, chandlery and books.

Cowroast lock.

Aylesbury

IN COMMON WITH the Northampton Arm, the Aylesbury Arm has the dubious distinction of featuring a considerable number of locks in a comparitively short distance. But the Aylesbury Arm's attraction lies not so much in the steepness of its gradient as in the tranquility of its setting. Once you have negotiated the staircase lock at Marsworth you are ravished by the immediate and utter intimacy of the arm, which proceeds to spill down into the Vale like an apple-cart rumbling along a country lane. In the fields bordering the canal pigs frolic in the mud and hens scrat for tasty morsels on a dung heap. For a couple of miles, the arm passes into Hertfordshire, but the landscape, if not its inhabitants, is aloof from local politics and disparities in Poll Tax, the inherent peace of the canal being broken only by the hooting of car horns as they approach each hump-backed bridge.

At this point you will probably be impatient for facts, even though, as Sir John Squire once ruefully pointed out, they are only flies in the amber. But the bare essentials are that the canal was promoted late in the 18th century as a through route across the Vale of Aylesbury to the Thames at Abingdon, from whence connection could be made via the Wilts & Berks and Kennet & Avon canals to Bath and Bristol. What a mouth-watering canal odyssey that would have made possible. However, only the arm to Aylesbury materialised, and following the opening in 1815, it settled down to a century and a half of trade, notably to and from Nestles condensed milk factory near the terminus of the arm and through the carrying activities of the well known boat company Harvey-Taylor.

Although the Aylesbury Arm is an essentially rural canal, there is much to see and discuss. Locks 1 and 2 – the staircase pair – are overlooked by British Waterways' section office. To the rear of their premises a small works manufactures concrete fencing. Interestingly, this once belonged to BW and was formerly used for the casting of concrete piling. As you proceed across the border into Herts there are views to the north of Mentmore, designed by Paxton for one of the Rothschilds but now occupied by Transcendentalists. Soon the flint tower of Marsworth church, backed by the tall

chimneys of Pitstone cement works and the scarp of the Ivinghoe Hills, is left astern and, as the gradient eases, the locks come less closely spaced. Red House lock is named after an isolated inn of the same name which stood alongside it, but which was converted into a private residence in the mid Sixties. Beyond here the channel narrows perceptibly and the reeds seem to whisper like conspirators as you pass.

Eventually the outskirts of Aylesbury begin to make themselves felt and you are treated to the surprisingly substantial and not entirely uninteresting industrial purlieus of the town: a snorting, humming metalworks; a big paperback book printing factory; a flour mill once served by the canal; and finally Nestles themselves, who naturally and sadly eschew carriage by canal now. Two demure lines of terraced houses, linked by a recently rebuilt footbridge, herald the L-shaped terminal basin with its friendly community of residential boats. The chances are you will be welcomed by a member of the local canal society and pointed politely to a suitable mooring in the shadow of the Inland Revenue office block which dominates the basin. Relax, overnight moorings are tax deductible.

Town Centre

Aylesbury Basin

Nestles Works

Akeman Street

industrial estate

Aylesbury Locks

industrial estate

Broughton Lock 14

Aston Clinton

Red House Lock 13

Buckland Lock 12

Bucks

Herts

LEICESTERSHIRE FOLK seem to regard Foxton Locks as their own personal street theatre. They descend on the famous flight in droves. Leaving their vehicles in the car park at the top, they stroll down to the pub, giving scant rein to their children's excitement, much to the chagrin of the lock-keeper who lives with the perpetual fear of tradgedy. The inland navigator plays a staring role in Foxton's soap opera, and is expected to respond cheerfully to bizarre questions and fatuous remarks with the amused tolerance of a Gulliver amidst Lilliputians.

That Foxton is a canal centre at all is due to historical accident. The original concept, dating from 1793, was for a canal to link Leicester with Northampton; connection southwards with the Grand Junction Canal would be made at the latter town. In the event, the Leicestershire & Northamptonshire Union Canal - built to broadbeam dimensions - ran out of capital and was forced to terminate for a dozen ignominious years at the village of Debdale, a couple of miles to the north of Foxton. Progress southwards as far as Market Harborough was completed in 1809, but the direct route to Northampton was never built. In exasperation, a new company was promoted to link the Leics & Northants with the Grand Junction. Known as the 'Grand Union', it charted a 23-mile route from Norton to Foxton, including two precipitous flights of narrowbeam locks ascending at either end of a 20-mile summit. The locks at Foxton consisted of two staircases of five chambers.

Thus the seeds were sown for Foxton's prominence. The village which had never been earmarked as a junction settled down to three-quarters of a century of fluctuating trade. The 'Grand Union' never made much profit and was bought out by the Grand Junction in 1894. Fellows, Morton & Clayton, the route's prime users, were by this time agitating for improvements to the bottle-neck staircases at Watford and Foxton and for a widening of the gauge. In what, with hindsight, can be seen an over-enthusiastic response, the Grand Junction proposed boat lifts, or more properly, inclined planes, at both sites. Only the one at Foxton was built, it opened in 1900. Archive photographs - and happily there seems to be no shortage of them - show us the astonishing grandeur of the inclined plane: an upper and lower dock, separated by a 1:4 gradient laid with rails, supporting two counterbalanced tanks each capable of taking a barge or pair of narrowboats. In the extremely informative booklet describing the plane, its history and operation, and admirable plans for restoration, the Foxton Inclined Plane Trust describe an imaginary journey through the lift; a ten minute ride replacing an hour on the locks. As an experience it must have been like travelling in a huge, open air funicular.

But for all their tub-thumping, FMC's trade never built to a level commensurate with the viable operation of the lift. Days were wont to go by when the attendants had nothing better to do than stoke the boiler and squirt oil on the moving parts: the railways had long since cornered the bulk of traffic between the East Midlands and London. Paradoxically, FMC and other carriers were irked that the lift was closed at night, occasioning delay to the 24 hour 'fly' boats which used the route. In response, the locks - unused since the opening of the lift - were reinstated and, inevitably, it was not long before these were deemed economically preferable to the lift, closure of which is recorded as having taken place in November 1910. The structure lay derelict through the years of the first world war, but was demolished in 1928 by a firm of Shropshire scrap merchants, who paid the princely sum of £250 for the privilege.

The Market Harborough Arm

The scheme for a through route to Northampton moribund, the canal between Foxton and Market Harborough lapsed into branch status, a character prevalent to this day. From the foot of Foxton Locks its sets off on its 5½ mile ramble, tenderly overlooked by the tower of the village church, like a fond mother seeing an only child off to school. The arm is rarely busy with boats, tending to attract only the inquisitive boater; the sort who like to poke their prow up the lonely backwaters of the system. Its route circles the skirts of Gallow Hill. To the north-east there are splendid vistas across the village-sprinkled valley of the River Welland. During the second world war they built a bomber base on the top of Gallow Hill, but the site is now occupied by Gartree Prison, a maximum security establishment whose high walls and floodlights can occasionally be glimpsed from the canal. Some years ago a prisoner made a daring escape in a helicopter landed within the prison compound by an accomplice. By bridge 8 there is a factory engaged in the unsavoury and occasionally noxious business of transforming old animal bones into meal and tallow for use in the manufacture, elsewhere, of animal feeds and soap. Otherwise, the arm is largely undisturbed and undemonstrative, finged with reeds, arrowhead and water lilies, its narrow channel measured, mile by mile, with the aid of simple iron mileposts counting the distance from Foxton.

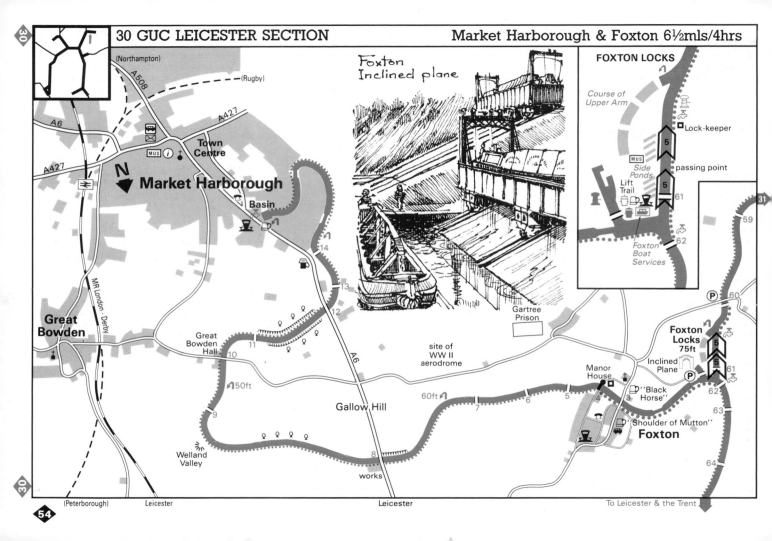

Foxton Inclined plane

FOXTON LOCKS

Course of Upper Arm

□ Lock-keeper

MUS *Side Ponds*

passing point

Lift Trail

Foxton Boat Services

(Northampton)

(Rugby)

A508

A6

A427

A427

MR London - Derby

N

Market Harborough

Town Centre

MUS ⓘ †

Basin

14

13

12

11

10

Great Bowden Hall

Great Bowden

†

50ft

9

Welland Valley

works

8

Gallow Hill

60ft

site of WW II aerodrome

A6

7

6

5

4

3 "Black Horse"

"Shoulder of Mutton"

Manor House

Inclined Plane

P

Foxton

Gartree Prison

Foxton Locks 75ft

P

5

5

61

62

63

64

59

60

61

62

(Peterborough) Leicester

Leicester

To Leicester & the Trent

Four miles out from Foxton the arm negotiates a wooded cutting with resident kingfishers. Then, passing beneath the now bypassed original course of the A6, it sinks gradually deeper and deeper into the suburban heart of 'Harboro; all lawns, laurels and lachrymose willows. If the foliage looks more established than the Sixties architecture, it is because the land on the outside of the canal formed the demesne of a large house long since demolished. Abruptly, but still in the land of flymos and barbecues, the canal expands in width to form its terminal basin. Having arrived, it is difficult to shake off the feeling that you are forty years too late. There is a shabby melancholy about the basin now that mocks at the gay scenes of 1950, when the fledgling Inland Waterways Association held their first festival here. Market Harborough was chosen for this auspicuous event because of its central location, its accessibility to wide-beam craft, and as it would not interfere with commercial carrying.

Market Harborough

All the quieter for its by-pass, Harborough remains a likeable town to visit, with some charming architectural interludes. Take, for example, Church Square, dominated by the parish church of St Dionysius with its soaring ashlar spire, but also containing a wonderfully picturesque timber building on stilts which was formerly the grammar school, and a handsome Victorian clothing mill. The town exudes a healthy vitality and is inherently good looking without being overtly conscious of it, whilst its hustle and bustle comes as a welcome palliative to the soporific charm of the Leicester Section.

Eating & Drinking
THE THREE SWANS - High Street. Comfortable bars and excellent restaurant. Worth making a pilgrimage to for the spirit of John Fothergill who wrote about it in his book "My Three Inns".
ELIOTS - High Street. Quaint cafe/restaurant next door to 'the Angel Hotel.

Shopping
Harborough boasts a profusion of charmingly individual shops such as SPENCERS the baker and cheese merchant in Church Street, BATES the butcher, HOBBS the fishmonger and TEMPTATIONS delicatessen in nearby Adam & Eve Street. The traders are mostly still old fashioned enough to honour Wednesday as a half day, whilst Tuesdays and Saturdays contrast with the hurly burly of an open market. The town centre is less than 10 minutes walk from the canal basin, but there is a handy newsagent and general store open daily on the main road opposite.

Things to Do
TOURIST INFORMATION - The Library, Adam & Eve Street. Tel: MH (0858) 462649.
HARBOROUGH MUSEUM - Adam & Eve Street. Tel: MH (0858) 432468. open daily, admission free. Interesting display of the town's past, including its stock in trade, the manufacture of corsetry.

Public Transport
BUSES - bus station on Northampton Road, but most services also call at stops along the High Street. Tel: Leicester (0533) 313391 for county timetable information relating to all operators services.
TRAINS - well served by Intercity trains between London and Leicester. Tel: Leicester (0533) 629811.

Foxton

Foxton village sits in the sun like a sleek cat that has just had two helpings of cream. Property prices here must average six figures, and on weekdays when the bread-winners are away it is as quiet as a nunnery. Up on their hilltop, the manor and church daydream of their fuedal past.

Eating & Drinking
BRIDGE 61 - canalside by bottom lock. Operated by the local boatyard and suitably decorated with canal artefacts and photographs of the lift in its glory. Open all day in the summer, restricted openings out of season.
BLACK HORSE - adjacent bridge 3. Ind Coope, bar meals, skittle alley, garden and Sunday lunches.
SHOULDER OF MUTTON - just north of bridge 3. Up market bar and restaurant meals but no facilities for children. Ruddles beers.

Shopping
The village is prosperous enough to retain its post office stores which are reasonably well stocked and sell newspapers. Early closing on Wednesdays and Saturdays and not open at all on Sundays. Provisions are also generally available from Foxton Boat Services' shop at the junction.

Things to Do
LIFT TRAIL & MUSEUM - waymarked path around the site of the inclined plane and interesting exhibits in former boiler house.
BOAT TRIPS - short horse drawn trips along the MH arm. Refer to boatyard.

Public Transport
BUSES - Midland Red Fox service 143 links Foxton with Market Harborough. The timetable cetainly isn't intensive, but if you plan ahead good enough to enable you to walk the Market Harborough Arm in one direction, using the bus in the other. Tel: Leicester (0533) 313391 for further details.

Boating Facilities
FOXTON BOAT SERVICES - Bottom Lock, Foxton, Market Harborough LE16 7RA. Tel: Leicester (0533) 792285. 4 and 6 berth hire craft bookable direct. Pumpout, diesel, petrol, water, Elsan & refuse disposal, Calor gas, long & short term moorings, repairs & servicing, sales & brokerage. Shop stocking groceries, gifts and chandlery; specialists in canal ware. Payphone.

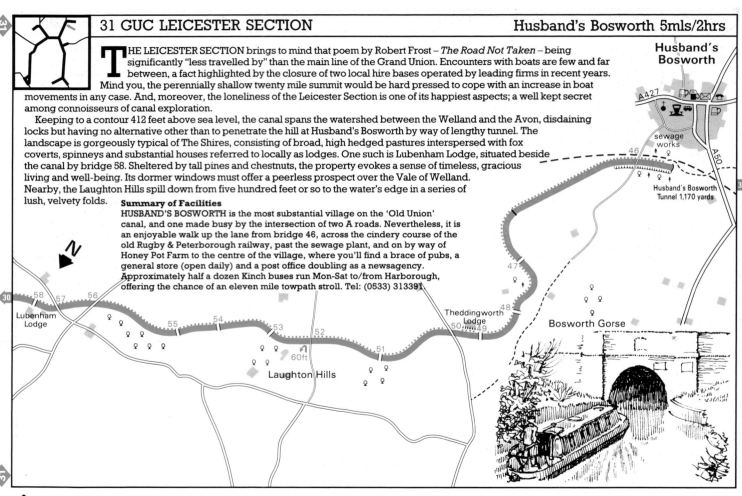

THE LEICESTER SECTION brings to mind that poem by Robert Frost – *The Road Not Taken* – being significantly "less travelled by" than the main line of the Grand Union. Encounters with boats are few and far between, a fact highlighted by the closure of two local hire bases operated by leading firms in recent years. Mind you, the perennially shallow twenty mile summit would be hard pressed to cope with an increase in boat movements in any case. And, moreover, the loneliness of the Leicester Section is one of its happiest aspects; a well kept secret among connoisseurs of canal exploration.

Keeping to a contour 412 feet above sea level, the canal spans the watershed between the Welland and the Avon, disdaining locks but having no alternative other than to penetrate the hill at Husband's Bosworth by way of lengthy tunnel. The landscape is gorgeously typical of The Shires, consisting of broad, high hedged pastures interspersed with fox coverts, spinneys and substantial houses referred to locally as lodges. One such is Lubenham Lodge, situated beside the canal by bridge 58. Sheltered by tall pines and chestnuts, the property evokes a sense of timeless, gracious living and well-being. Its dormer windows must offer a peerless prospect over the Vale of Welland. Nearby, the Laughton Hills spill down from five hundred feet or so to the water's edge in a series of lush, velvety folds.

Summary of Facilities
HUSBAND'S BOSWORTH is the most substantial village on the 'Old Union' canal, and one made busy by the intersection of two A roads. Nevertheless, it is an enjoyable walk up the lane from bridge 46, across the cindery course of the old Rugby & Peterborough railway, past the sewage plant, and on by way of Honey Pot Farm to the centre of the village, where you'll find a brace of pubs, a general store (open daily) and a post office doubling as a newsagency. Approximately half a dozen Kinch buses run Mon-Sat to/from Harborough, offering the chance of an eleven mile towpath stroll. Tel: (0533) 313391.

Husband's
Bosworth

A427

A50

sewage
works

46

Husband's Bosworth
Tunnel 1,170 yards

32

47

Theddingworth
Lodge

48

50   49

Bosworth Gorse

30

58   57   56

Lubenham
Lodge

55   54

53

52

60ft

51

Laughton Hills

N

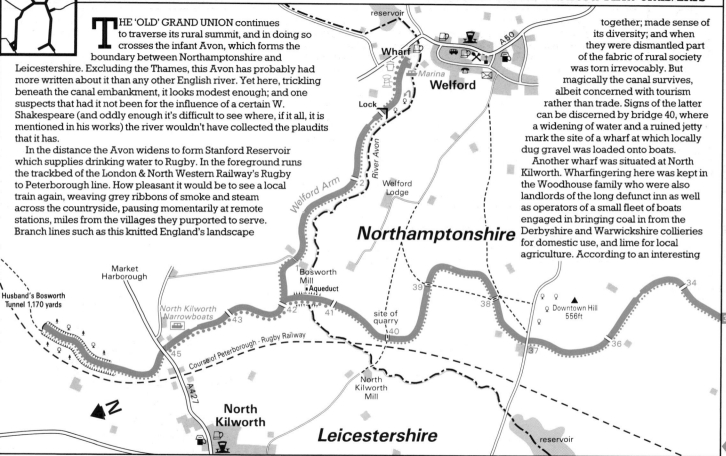

THE 'OLD' GRAND UNION continues to traverse its rural summit, and in doing so crosses the infant Avon, which forms the boundary between Northamptonshire and Leicestershire. Excluding the Thames, this Avon has probably had more written about it than any other English river. Yet here, trickling beneath the canal embankment, it looks modest enough; and one suspects that had it not been for the influence of a certain W. Shakespeare (and oddly enough it's difficult to see where, if it all, it is mentioned in his works) the river wouldn't have collected the plaudits that it has.

In the distance the Avon widens to form Stanford Reservoir which supplies drinking water to Rugby. In the foreground runs the trackbed of the London & North Western Railway's Rugby to Peterborough line. How pleasant it would be to see a local train again, weaving grey ribbons of smoke and steam across the countryside, pausing momentarily at remote stations, miles from the villages they purported to serve. Branch lines such as this knitted England's landscape

together; made sense of its diversity; and when they were dismantled part of the fabric of rural society was torn irrevocably. But magically the canal survives, albeit concerned with tourism rather than trade. Signs of the latter can be discerned by bridge 40, where a widening of water and a ruined jetty mark the site of a wharf at which locally dug gravel was loaded onto boats.

Another wharf was situated at North Kilworth. Wharfingering here was kept in the Woodhouse family who were also landlords of the long defunct inn as well as operators of a small fleet of boats engaged in bringing coal in from the Derbyshire and Warwickshire collieries for domestic use, and lime for local agriculture. According to an interesting

Map labels

reservoir

Wharf

Marina

Welford

Lock

River Avon

Welford Arm

Welford Lodge

42

Northamptonshire

31

Husband's Bosworth Tunnel 1,170 yards

Market Harborough

Bosworth Mill

Aqueduct

North Kilworth Narrowboats

43   42   41

45

Course of Peterborough - Rugby Railway

North Kilworth Mill

North Kilworth

Rugby

39

site of quarry

40

38

37   36

Downtown Hill 556ft

34

33

Leicestershire

reservoir

South Kilworth

A50

A427

Figures refer to main line, allow an hour in each direction for the arm.

booklet produced by the Old Union Canal Society one of the Woodhouse boats was contracted to carry scrap when the inclined plane at Foxton was being demolished, but its back was broken under the weight of the load and it sank at the foot of the flight. L.T.C. Rolt mentions the inn in "Narrow Boat". to the north of the wharf, and the busy A427, the canal winds through a deep, tree-bowered cutting to the portal of Husband's Bosworth tunnel.

The Welford Arm

Not so much an arm, more a finger, the branch was dug to bring water from Welford, Sulby and Naseby reservoirs to feed the main line. But a certain amount of trade developed and coal was still being brought in by boat at the end of the second world war; Joe and Rose Skinner being occasional traders here. Thereafter the arm fell into decay, and though still being used as a feeder, was allowed to silt up. It remained unnavigable for over twenty years until its re-opening in 1969.

Leaving the main line, the arm establishes its individuality by dint of its overbridges being numbered from one upwards. Furthermore, the adjacent ridges close in to create a feeling of intimacy in contrast with the panoramic views offered by the rest of the Leicester Section. After a mile the arm rises through a diminutive lock to reach 417 feet, the highest pound on the whole of the former Grand Union system. The terminus is just around the corner. Since we were last here a marina has been dug out, and is now well filled with private craft.

A detour up the Welform Arm is difficult to resist. Boaters are, by definition, explorers at heart, and the end of the arm makes a pleasant overnight mooring with the facilities of the village and the wildlife of the reservoirs near at hand. The country writer 'BB' (aka Denys Watkins Pitchford, who illustrated "Narrow Boat") included several passages describing flora and fauna of the Welford Arm in his book "The Wayfaring Tree".

North Kilworth

Traffic-swept settlement on the A427, not as handily placed for canal users as Husband's Bosworth.

Boating Facilities

ANGLO-WELSH - Kilworth Marina. 4 to 8 berth hire craft. Tel: Market Harborough (0858) 466910.
NORTH KILWORTH NARROW BOATS - Kilworth Marina, Lutterworth, LE17 6JB. Tel: Market Harborough (0858) 880484. Pumpout, diesel, water, Elsan & refuse disposal, Calor & Shell gas, long term moorings for craft up to 26ft, slipway, repairs & servicing, boatbuilding and fitting-out, drydock with DIY facilities, hard storage, shop with groceries, off-licence, chandlery and gifts.

Welford

Attractive village strung out along the A50 - keep a weather eye open for the traffic if you walk into the centre from the wharf.

Eating & Drinking

WHARF INN - adjacent canal terminus. Bar meals and Sunday lunches.
SWAN INN - village centre. Marstons, bar meals, families welcome.
SHOULDER OF MUTTON - village centre. Les Routiers recommended pub. Ruddles, bar meals, garden.
THE ELIZABETHAN RESTAURANT - High Street. Tel: MH (0858) 575311.

Shopping

MACE general stores and newsagency on High Street open daily early to late. Post office also selling newspapers near church. Calor gas available from garage at top of High Street.

Public Transport

BUSES - Kinch coaches to/from Market Harborough approx 4 each way Mon-Sat. Tel: Leicester (0533) 313391.

Boating Facilities

WELFORD MARINA - Tel: Market Harborough (0858) 575995. Long term moorings and general services.

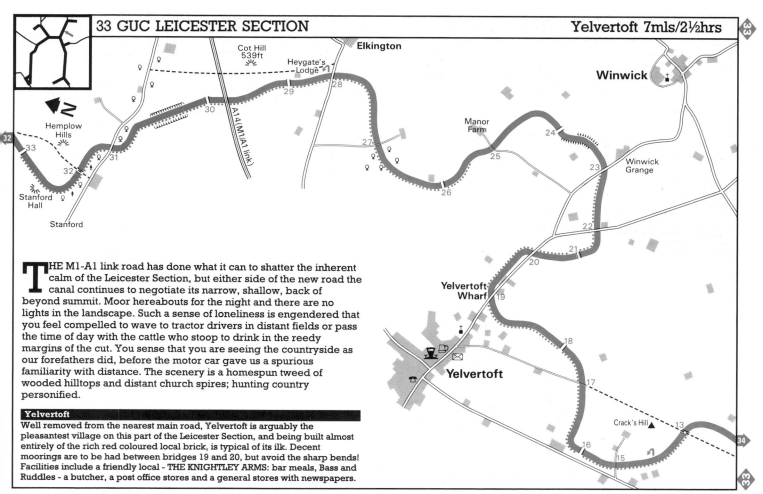

THE M1-A1 link road has done what it can to shatter the inherent calm of the Leicester Section, but either side of the new road the canal continues to negotiate its narrow, shallow, back of beyond summit. Moor hereabouts for the night and there are no lights in the landscape. Such a sense of loneliness is engendered that you feel compelled to wave to tractor drivers in distant fields or pass the time of day with the cattle who stoop to drink in the reedy margins of the cut. You sense that you are seeing the countryside as our forefathers did, before the motor car gave us a spurious familiarity with distance. The scenery is a homespun tweed of wooded hilltops and distant church spires; hunting country personified.

Yelvertoft

Well removed from the nearest main road, Yelvertoft is arguably the pleasantest village on this part of the Leicester Section, and being built almost entirely of the rich red coloured local brick, is typical of its ilk. Decent moorings are to be had between bridges 19 and 20, but avoid the sharp bends! Facilities include a friendly local - THE KNIGHTLEY ARMS: bar meals, Bass and Ruddles - a butcher, a post office stores and a general stores with newspapers.

THE CANAL, railway, and two generations of main road plunge through a gap in the hills between the villages of Ashby St Ledgers and Watford. By now you will be beginning to realise that you get nowhere fast on the Leicester Section, but as there isn't anywhere particular to go this barely seems to matter. Watford Locks come as a rude interruption to any incipient daydreaming, however, for here you need exercise not only your muscles but your mind as well.

In their Cruising Guide published in the early Sixties, British Waterways devoted three pages of text and diagrams to the recommended operational techniques at Watford and Foxton lock flights. The information included up to eighteen specific instructions depending on whether the locks were set with or against you. Gates were allocated key letters from A to E, paddles from S to Z. The man who wrote the text was later employed by the Inland Revenue designing end of year tax return forms.

Nowadays the locks are generally manned and the lock-keeper will be happy to explain their operation.

Watford Locks raise the Leicester Section 52½ feet to its summit level of 412 feet. They are picturesquely bordered by a spinney of ash, chestnut and beech which screen them from the motorway. The central four chambers are in the form of a staircase which, with their balance beams and tail bridges look like a group of grimacing acrobats. At the turn of the century there were plans to replace the flight with an inclined plane like that at Foxton, but the scheme was shelved. When the Grand Union was formed in 1929 there were further proposals for the flight to be improved by widening, but these also languished.

Above the locks, and once clear of the M1, the Leicester Section quickly establishes its character as a reclusive waterway, painfully shy when it comes to encounters with villages *en route*. As our research crew found to their cost, it pays to have both the galley and the kitty full before setting off into the unknown. Crick Tunnel is almost a mile long and, in common with the other two tunnels on the Leicester Section, doesn't have a towpath. In the old days the boat horses found their way over the top, a bygone aspect of village life in Crick recalled by te naming of a residential street, Boathorse Lane.

Boating Facilities

JUST BOATS – Crick Wharf, Crick, Northampton NW6 7XT. Tel: Crick (0788) 822793. Pumpout, diesel, water, Elsan disposal, Shell gas, moorings, repairs and servicing, boatbuilding and fitting out, sales and brokerage.

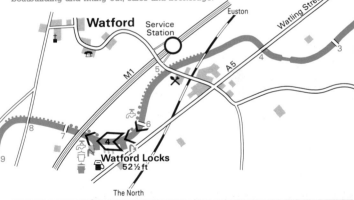

Watford

Extremely pretty estate village which has somehow survived construction of the M1 past its back door, though the big house, Watford Court, was demolished to escape death taxes. No shop now, but there is surreptitious access from bridge 5 into the motorway service station if you're in dire straits. The STAG'S HEAD, canalside by bridge 6, is primarily a restaurant, though it has a public bar.

Crick

Useful watering-hole, but otherwise unremarkable village set about a crossroads on the Rugby – Northampton road. Post office stores adjacent to bridge 12, plus a Co-op further into the village. Three pubs in the centre, but an attractive eatery – EDWARD'S – canalside, offering informal or restaurant meals; closed all day Mondays and Sunday evenings.

Information

There are thirty-four numbered maps. Maps 1 to 16 cover the Oxford Canal; maps 17 to 29 cover the Grand Union from Braunston to Berkhamsted and Aylesbury; maps 30 to 34 cover the Leicester Section between Market Harborough and Norton Junction. All the maps can be used equally well in either direction. Generally speaking, travelling south you should read them left to right - travelling north, right to left. The simplest way of progressing from map to map is to proceed to the next map numbered from the edge of the map you are on. A 'thumbnail' diagram at the top left hand corner of each map indicates your overall position in respect of the adjoining waterways covered in this guide. Figures quoted at the top of each map relate to distance and average cruising time for that page. An alternative indication of time can be found on the Route Planner on the inside front cover. Obviously cruising times can vary depending on the nature of your boat and the number of crew at your disposal, so quoted times should only be taken as an estimate.

Using the Text

Each map is accompanied by a route commentary describing the landscape and placing the canal in its historical context. Details of most settlements passed through are given together with itemised or summarised information on facilities.

Eating & Drinking. Pubs, restaurants, cafes, fish & chip shops and fast-food outlets considered to be of interest to canal users are listed. In towns and cities a selection has obviously to be made and we try to list a cross-section of establishments likely to appeal to differing tastes and budgets. We don't set out to make judgements in an 'egon ronay' sense, but generally speaking, the more detail we give, the higher in esteem any particular establishment is likely to be held. By the very nature of their trade, pubs and restaurants tend to change hands, alter services, or simply close down, and we apologise in advance for any inaccurate or misleading entries in the text.

Shopping. Shopping in unfamiliar towns and villages is one of the lesser-sung pleasures of canal travel. We have consciously expanded our coverage of shopping facilities, giving any mention to any unusual, quirky, charming, or simply timeless shops worth patronising for the experience alone.

Places to Visit. Details are given in this category of Tourist Information Centres, museums, stately homes etc likely to be of interest to canal users.

Public Transport. Information in this category is quoted particularly for the benefit of walkers who wish to walk along the towpath 'one-way', using a bus or train in the opposite direction. In such instances do take the trouble to telephone and check up to date details of the service.

Boating Facilties. Every boatyard and hire base is marked on the relevant map and listed appropriately. It is not practical for us to quote any indication of quality and cost applicable to individual fleets, and we would recommend that prospective hirers obtain a selection of brochures from hire operators and agencies such as Hoseasons before booking.

Walking

Towpaths are the property of British Waterways and, though not specifically 'rights of way', are open to the general public, no licence or permit being required for their use by walkers. Cyclists, however, are not allowed to ride along towpaths without an annual licence, priced £3 and obtainable from BW offices. Much has been done in recent years - usually in association with local authorities and other public bodies - to improve towpath conditions and increase public access and we have tried to reflect this in the three categories we depict the towpath with on the maps. Thus 'good' can usually be taken to indicate the existence of a firm, wide and dry base suitable for comfortable walking and cycling. 'Adequate' hints at the chance of mud and vegetation not conducive to cycling, but usually feasible for walking. 'Poor' or 'non-existent' speaks for itself; diehards may get through, but it won't be much fun!

Boating

Boating on inland waterways is an established, though relatively small facet of the UK holiday industry. There are over 20,000 privately owned boats registered on the canals. In addition to this numerous firms offer boats for hire; the canal equivalent of a self-catering cottage. Boat hire companies range in size from small operators with half a dozen boats to sizeable fleets run by concerns with several bases.

Most boats have all the creature comforts you are likely to expect. In the excitement of planning a boating holiday you may give scant thought to the inventory and decor of your hire boat, but at the end of a hard day's boating such things take on more significance. A well equipped and reliable boat can make or break a holiday.

Traditionally hire boats are booked out by the week or fortnight, but an increasing number of firms advertise short break holidays of two, three or four days duration. All reputable hire firms give newcomers tuition in boat handling, lock working and general navigation, and first-timers soon find themselves adapting to the pace of things 'on the cut'.

Canal boating holidays are enjoyed by many thousands of people every year. As a holiday activity it can become compulsive. Many hire firms find their customers coming back year after year, only losing them when they can no longer resist the temptation to buy a boat of their own!

Navigational Advice

Locks. Locks are part of the fun of boating, but they are potentially dangerous places for careless adults, children and pets. Use of them should be methodical and unhurried. Special care should be taken in rain, frost and snow when slippery hazards abound.

The locks included in this guide fall into three distinct types: wide and narrow canal locks and river locks. Wide-beam canal locks are to be found on the main line of the Grand Union Canal between Braunston and Berkhamsted. These locks are wide enough to accept narrowbeam craft side by side, and it helps save water and work if you can share them with other boats. Turbulence can be a problem in these larger chambers when travelling uphill, and you may find that a rope cast round the lockside bollards usually provided will reduce this. Another worthwhile tip in this situation, if you are travelling alone, is to open the ground paddle on the same side as your boat first, which will help to keep the boat against the wall of the lock, preventing it from crashing about as the water floods in.

The Oxford Canal, Leicester Section of the Grand Union and Aylesbury Arm all feature narrowbeam locks of traditional pattern. They have their idiosyncracies of course (like the flights at Watford and Foxton which are linked to extended side ponds) but generally speaking present no difficulties in operation. One or two locks on the Oxford Canal are constructed to an unusual 'diamond' shape, but they are operated in the usual way.

River locks are encountered on the alternative approach to Oxford via the Duke's Cut. Osney, Godstow and Kings locks are manned and it is the practice here to make fast bow and stern and switch off your boat's engine. As the water rises or falls lines must be adjusted accordingly. Lock-keeper's hours of duty are displayed at each lock.

Lift Bridges. The Oxford Canal features numerous lift bridges but the majority of them remain open to boats except for when being used, mostly by local farmers to gain access from one field to another. The moral is to 'leave them as you find them.'

Closures. Closures - known as 'stoppages' on the canals - usually occur between November and April when maintenance work is undertaken. Occasionally, however, an emergency stoppage may be imposed at short notice, closing part of the route you intend to cruise. Up to date details are usually available from hire bases. Private boat owners can telephone British Waterways recorded message service on 071-723 8487 for up to date details.

Societies

The Inland Waterways Association was founded in 1946 to campaign for retention of the canal system. Many of the routes now open to pleasure boaters now might not have been available but for this organisation. Several of the individual canals featured in this guide have their own support groups as well. Details of these and more information on the IWA itself can be obtained from: Inland Waterways Association, 114 Regent's Park Road, London NW1 8UQ. Tel: 071-586 2556.

Useful Contacts

Waterway Managers are responsible for individual sections of canal. They welcome enquiries from the general public, either in person or by telephone. The offices relevant to the canals covered by this guide are as follows:

Oxford Canal/ Grand Union Canal
(north of Stowe Hill)
British Waterways
Braunston
Northants
NN11 7JQ
Tel: Rugby (0788) 890666

Grand Union Canal
(south of Stowe Hill)
British Waterways
Watery Lane
Marsworth
HP23 4LZ
Tel: Tring (044282) 5938

Acknowledgements
Brian Collings executed the cover in a style not unlike Samuel Barlow. All internal sketches were done by Eric Leslie. Malcolm Barnes did the cartography from our own personal surveys whilst Les Robinson and Wendy Anderson sailed up the Leicester Line on our behalf. Thanks to Alvechurch Boat Centres for the research boat, and to all at Character Graphics and J. H. Haynes for transmuting our dreams into reality.

THRUPP

Pearson's Canal Companion

KENNET & AVON
MIDDLE THAMES

Published by Central Waterways Supplies
of Rugby. Tel/fax 01788 546692

First edition 2003. ISBN 0 907864 97 X
Printed by STIGE of Turin, Italy.

tillerman

Five years is a long gestation period for a guidebook, even by Pearson Canal Companion standards. The reasons - though not excuses - behind this delay are too complicated to go in to here, but by the time the work was re-started for the umpteenth time, it was necessary, more or less, to do it all again to ensure continuity and topicality. The result - herewith modestly submitted for public approbation - fills perhaps the most obvious gap in the Pearson canon, and no longer will embarrassment follow telephone enquiries as to the availability of a guide to the Kennet & Avon.

It made sense to also cover the Thames between Oxford and Reading in this guide so as to provide a link with our Oxford & Grand Union Canal Companion. Further coverage, upstream and downstream, is likely to follow in due course of 'Pearson' time.

Finally, it has to be said, that for a guide book compiler who cut his teeth on the canals of the Midlands and the North, exploration of the waterways contained within proved revelatory. The Kennet & Avon is an astonishingly beautiful navigation, an enchanting mix of canal and river sections, whilst the Thames - inexplicably losing popularity in recent years - had your author in raptures each time he returned from a fresh research trip. Fickle man, what credibility will he have on the BCN now !

Michael Pearson

David Alison

Caen Hill Locks, Devizes

HILPERTON MARINA

Home of

Wessex Narrowboats

* Boatbuilding

* Boat Repairs

* BSS Centre

* Fast Dry Dock

* Slipway

* Corgi Gas

* Dayboat Hire

* Luxury Holiday Fleet

* Temporary Moorings

* Pump Out

* Diesel / Gas / Coal

* Boat Brokerage

Dutch Barge & Narrowboat Building

Well Stocked One-Stop-Chandlery for Canal Boating on the K & A

Breakdown Call-Out Service

Hilperton Marina, (Bridge 167), Trowbridge BA14 8RS Tel: 01225 765243 Fax: 01225 765243   www.wessexboats.co.uk e-mail: chandlery@wessexboats.co.uk

ENVY the lucky boater who has to begin or end their voyage in the superbly atmospheric setting of Bristol's Floating Harbour. Of course it's the vessels which 'float' and not the docks. Early in the 19th century William Jessop designed a new enclosed harbour to eradicate difficulties involved in loading and unloading vessels at the mercy of the River Avon's considerable tides. But Bristol's maritime tradition goes back much further than this, and many a fortune was acquired in the 'triangular trade': guns to Africa, slaves to America, sugar, rum, tobacco and cotton back. Coastal trade was an important tradition as well. The quayside at Welsh Back, now reminiscent of Amsterdam in its cobbled, tree-lined ambience, once reverberated to the clamour of Welsh voices whose owners had sailed over in trows with cargoes of slate and stone and coal. Beyond Bristol Bridge the now defunct brewery was formerly a busy user of water transport as well, and the importing of sherry was another activity closely associated with the port of Bristol. Trade ceased in the Floating Harbour in the 1970s but you can enjoyably investigate its origins and heyday by visiting the Industrial Museum,

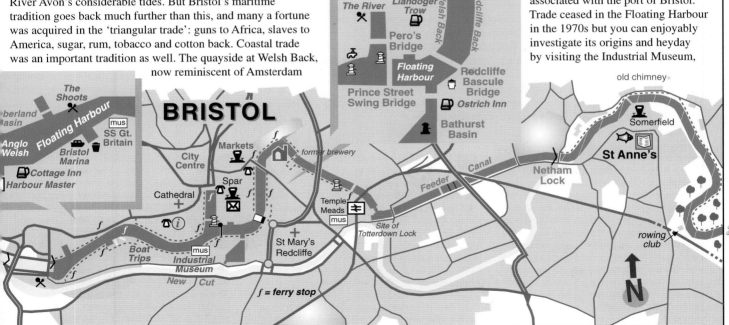

or by journeying over its broad waters on board one of the frequent ferries which operate all the way from Temple Quay in the east (adjacent to Temple Meads railway station) to Cumberland Basin in the west (by the entrance lock to the tidal Avon). The best public moorings for visiting boaters are to be found just west of Prince Street Swing Bridge. They offer handy and rapid access to the city centre. Both Prince Street and the neighbouring Redcliffe Bascule Bridge offer sufficient headroom for most inland waterway craft without needing to be swung or raised respectively.

Walkways more or less intact on either bank permit pedestrian exploration of the Floating Harbour. By the Industrial Museum, in an area known as Wapping Wharf, railway tracks bearing preserved wagons remain in situ creating an atmosphere of days gone by when much transhipment occurred. Sadly all the lines have been uprooted on the opposite side of the harbour where signs used to advise drivers to desist from shunting during periods when services were being held in the adjoining Cathedral.

How nice it would be to return to those days. In the mid Fifties something in the region of ten thousand ships per annum were visiting the Port of Bristol, though the larger vessels involved used the docks at Portishead and Avonmouth as their tonnage precluded passage upstream through the restrictive Avon Gorge where the tidal range was close to fifty feet. The City Docks hosted the coastal and Continental trade, vessels up to a maximum of about fifteen hundred tons. Many traded from the Baltic and Scandinavia with timber and woodpulp for Bristol's paper-makers. From warmer climes came wine from Portugal, Spanish grapefruits and South African oranges. However colourful, today's pleasure craft, and the little fleet of interesting vessels which form part of the Industrial Museum's collection, and even the mighty SS *Great Britain* itself, seem small consolation for the busy past.

Passing beneath the phalanx of railway tracks which form the northern approach to Temple Meads station, boaters make their way out of the city along the Feeder Canal as far as Netham Lock. This is not a particularly salubrious part of the city in terms of general appearance. Depending on tide levels, Netham Lock may well be open to pass through without operating. Beyond it steer well clear of the weir which takes the Avon downstream towards the open sea. Useful shopping facilities are available at St Anne's, though you may have to improvise when mooring and this is definitely not a spot for a lengthy stay.

Bristol (Map 1)

Hometown of such disparate characters as John Cabot, Isambard Kingdom Brunel and Cary Grant, Bristol is a terrific city, full of atmospheric passages and corners, alleyways and stairways as befits a former sea-trading port. Though much damage was brought about by bombing raids during the Second World War, a sense of unity has been restored and the melding of old and new has been more successful here than in say Plymouth or Coventry for instance. Two magnificent churches cry out for your attention, the Cathedral and St Mary's, Redcliffe. Elizabeth I described the latter as the fairest church in England.

THE RIVER - Watershed. Tel: 0117 930 0498. Classic homemade British cuisine with a waterside setting.
GLASS BOAT - Welsh Back. Tel: 0117 929 0704. Floating restaurant of considerable appeal by Bristol Bridge. Breakfasts, lunches, dinners.
THE SHOOTS - Hotwells Road (north bank of Floating Harbour) Tel: 0117 925 0597. Another excellent floating restaurant.
SAN CARLO - Corn Street. Tel: 0117 922 6586. Upmarket Italian chain restaurant.
LLANDOGER TROW - King Street. Tel: 0870 7001342. 17th century inn named after a village on the Wye which regularly traded with Bristol, thought to be the 'Spyglass Inn' of Stevenson's *Treasure Island.* Now a Premier Lodge.
BREWERY TAP - Colston Street. Tel: 0117 921 3668. There's a nice unspoilt feel to this pub which serves Smiles Bristol brewed ales.
HOWARDS RESTAURANT - Avon Crescent, Hotwells (by Cumberland Basin) Tel: 0117 926 2921.

Beat a path to ST NICHOLAS MARKETS, reminiscent of Oxford's wonderful indoor market, you'll find them just north of Bristol Bridge They meet their antithesis in the nearby BROADMEAD shopping centre. CHRISTMAS STEPS & ST MICHAEL'S is an imaginative shopping quarter in the vicinity of Colston Street.

i TOURIST INFORMATION - Harbourside. Tel: 0117 915 5000.

BRISTOL FERRY BOAT CO - Tel: 0117 927 3416. Commendably frequent services (including an all year round commuter operation supported by the city council) make the ferries an ideal way of seeing much of the city if you haven't brought your own boat with you.

INDUSTRIAL MUSEUM - Princes Wharf. Tel: 0117 925 1470. Bristol's seafaring past and other local trades paid homage to.

CLIFTON SUSPENSION BRIDGE VISITOR CENTRE - Sion Place. Tel: 0117 974 4664. Surprise, surprise, Brunel's wonderful bridge took thirty years from conception to completion, delayed by financial problems, social riots and indecision. Learn all this and more before going to see the bridge itself.

SS GREAT BRITAIN - Great Western Dockyard. Tel: 0117 929 1843. Brunel's first great ocean liner built in 1843. The museum also provides an occasional home to a working replica of John Cabot's *Matthew* in which he crossed the Atlantic and bumped into Newfoundland in 1497.

BRITISH EMPIRE & COMMONWEALTH MUSEUM - Temple Meads. Tel: 0117 925 4983. The rise and fall of the British Empire and its sphere of influence housed in Brunel's original Bristol railway station of 1840. Thoroughly recommended.

CITY MUSEUM & ART GALLERY - Queen's Road. Tel: 0117 922 3571.

@BRISTOL - Harbourside. Tel: 0845 345 1235. Multi-disciplined, 'hands on' visitor centre.

ARNOLFINI - Narrow Quay. Tel: 0117 929 9191. Renowned centre for contemporary arts.

BUSES - Tel: 0117 955 3231.
TRAINS - Tel: 08457 484950. Useful local services via Keynsham to Bath and beyond.

Hanham *(Map 2)*

OLD LOCK & WEIR - riverside. Tel: 0117 967 3793. Unspoilt CAMRA recommended pub featured in Conan Doyle's adventure *Micah Clark*. Moorings for patrons.

CHEQUERS - riverside. Tel: 0117 967 4242. So close to its neighbour (above) that there's really no excuse for not trying both. Slightly smarter perhaps. Customer moorings.

Keynsham *(Map 2)*

Surely no child of the Sixties can ever think of Keynsham and not hear Horace Batchelor slowly ennunciating the way to spell it on Radio Luxembourg. Further nostalgia emanates from the chocolate factory, originally erected by Frys of 'Five Boys' bar fame. Do you remember their faces? : desperation, expectation, realisation, pacification and acclamation! In the 1920s the works employed almost five thousand and a model housing estate was built for them called Somerdale. Much automated, the workforce is down to around six hundred now and the factory trades under the blurred brand name of Cadbury, Trebor, Bassett. In reality Keynsham is a surprisingly large town on the River Chew landmarked by the impressive 17th century tower of its parish church St John the Baptist. Legends surround a local Romano-British princess St Keyna who reputedly turned the neighbourhood's snakes to stone through the efficacy of prayer. A waymarked 'Mosaic Trail' illustrates aspects of local history, descriptive leaflets available from the library.

LOCK KEEPER - by Keynsham Lock. Tel: 0117 986 2383. Bristol-brewed Smiles and food.

THE BRASSMILL - near Keynsham Lock. Tel: 0117 986 7280. Brewers Fayre all day family pub and restaurant. Abraham Darby opened the original mill here early in the 18th century before making his name and fortune at Coalbrookdale in Shropshire. The mill continued commercially until as recently as 1927. During the First World War it produced shells for the British army.

Plenty of shops and banks etc in the town centre less than ten minutes walk from the Avon via the railway station.

TRAINS - Tel: 08457 484950. Useful local services to Bath and Bristol.

Saltford *(Map 3)*

Snug village of quiet by-roads away from the A4. The Manor house is of Norman origin. Handel is said to have been rhythmically inspired by the hammers in Saltford Brass Mill.

JOLLY SAILOR - by Saltford Lock. Tel: 01225 873002. Popular waterside inn offering a good range of food. Customer moorings.

BIRD IN HAND - High Street. Tel: 01225 873335. Well worth the stroll up from the river if only for a game of petanque in the garden overlooking the Bristol-Bath cycleway, but a convivial atmosphere inside and good food.

THE RIVERSIDE - overlooking Kelston Lock. Tel: 01225 873862. Modern restaurant pub developed with adjacent marina. Wadworth beers and a wide range of food. Customer moorings.

Useful (if not extensive) range of shops on A4 - chemist, Co-op, newsagent, post office etc. Thai and Chinese take-aways also.

SPRING tides occasionally lick their salty tongue up as far as Keynsham, but for the most part, other than after heavy rain, the Avon is pliant enough and the only boating hazards are the weirs which would draw the unwary away from the lock channels.

Scenically the landscape pivots on Hanham: to the east the valley is wide and watermeadowy; to the west wooded and gorge-like. Few buildings are foolhardy enough to encroach too closely upon the mercurial river, but here and there lies evidence of old industries which once needed to be near to the river because they relied upon it for transport: a boatbuilding company occupies premises - conspicuously dated 1881 - formerly used as a soap works; a weigh bridge office remains at Londonderry Wharf where coal was once loaded on to barges; Hanham Colliery once stood in what is now woodland on the north bank of the river downstream of the high A4174 road crossing; an old copper smelting chimney overlooks the river as it winds past the now domestic entrails of St Anne's Park where board mills and a tar distillery provided river trade up until the 1960s. Cadbury's chocolate factory at Keynsham dates from the 1920s but has the look of a Lancashire textile mill. On Keynsham Hams the beginning of the end for the Monmouth Rebellion took place in 1685 when the Duke of Beaufort's Cavalry routed the rebels prior to the bloody denouement at Sedgemoor. The imposing 17th century tower of Keynsham's parish church looms over the high embankment which carries the railway over the meadowlands.

Conham

Hanham Green

Bitton

Avon Valley Railway Bristol & Bath Railway Path

ferry

A4174

Hanham Court

Avon Walkway

Old Lock & Weir

The Chequers

WEIR !

Hanham Lock

Londonderry Wharf

Keynsham Hams

chocolate factory

A4175

Avon Valley Country Park

former soap works

Tidal Limit

Keynsham Lock

The Lock Keeper

The Brassmill

Portavon Marina

WEIR !

R. Chew

Co-op

Keynsham

Town Centre

A4

A4

THE River Avon shares its journey between Bristol and Bath with the A4 trunk road, the Great Western main line, and the course of the old Midland Railway which has been reborn as the "Bristol & Bath Railway Path", one of the earliest Sustrans projects which have brought admirable new use to abandoned railways; though, nostalgically, one might be forgiven for day-dreaming that your boat might be overtaken at any moment by the Pines Express! Beyond the valley floor, however, your focus is apt to be drawn to the rolling hills which fill the northern horizon. With time on your hands, and having secured suitable moorings (something at a premium on the Avon)

you might rewardingly essay a walk or two in this direction. Not that the river lacks inherent interest as it meanders from lock to lock, though one or two of its tighter bends have been ironed-out in recent times to lessen the threat of flooding.

One of the most potent images on this section of your journey is the ivy clad annealing ovens that are remnants of Kelston's former brass mill. They overlook the river by Saltford Lock and date from early in the 18th century when the mill employed the power of the Avon in the shaping of metal. There was also a brass mill at Swineford.

The mile long straight above Kelston Lock is used as a training reach by rowers- beware their wash!

The A4 elegantly crosses the river at New Bridge. The three railway bridges have less aesthetic value, but at least they provide pedestrians with the opportunity to cross the river in the regrettable absence of former ferries.

Three busy boatyards create considerable traffic on a stretch of inland waterway not readily associated with a high percentage of boating activity.

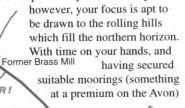

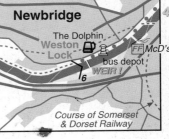

THE beautiful city of Bath plays host to the meeting of the Avon Navigation and the Kennet & Avon Canal. Arguably, only York and Chester, on the inland waterways system, can muster such an appealing backdrop, so architecturally delicious a dessert with which to finish off a fine day's boating. Morning, may bring, however be warned, a reluctance to cast off from your moorings, for there is so much to be seen and to be done that the canal's implicit siren call will need to be balanced against the city's inherent attractions.

The Avon is actually navigable for a short distance upstream of the canal's junction with the river at the tail of Bath Bottom (or Widcombe) Lock. It's a detour well worth making, for you may, space permitting, be fortunate enough to find moorings within sight of Pulteney Bridge, a peerless setting by any criteria.

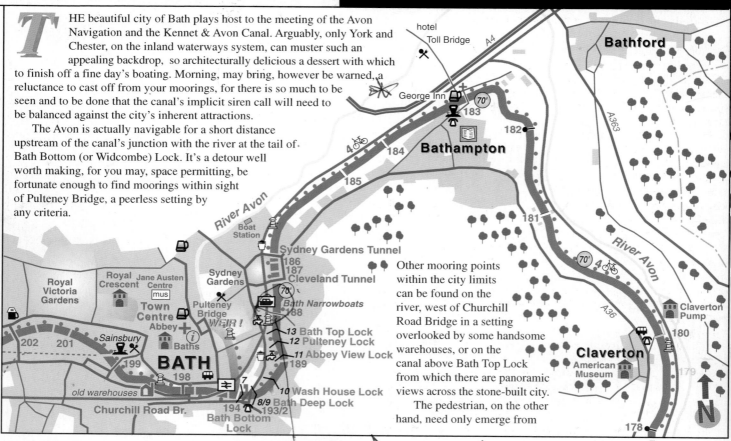

Other mooring points within the city limits can be found on the river, west of Churchill Road Bridge in a setting overlooked by some handsome warehouses, or on the canal above Bath Top Lock from which there are panoramic views across the stone-built city.

The pedestrian, on the other hand, need only emerge from

Bath Spa railway station (for no Pearson aficionado would be crass enough to come by car!) to find his or her way on to the towpath by way of Halfpenny Footbridge after which it's a simple heads or tails choice between exploring the river to the west or the canal to the east.

The River Avon

The River Avon plunges over Pulteney Weir before establishing its navigable status. Boating of a sort can, however, be enjoyed in a traditionally Victorian manner by repairing to Bath Boat Station, half a mile or so upstream, from where punts, skiffs and canoes can be hired for decorous exploration of the upper reaches.

Trip boats ply their trade downstream of Pulteney Weir as the river wends its way past Bath Rugby Club's well known Recreation Ground on one bank and the elegant Parade Gardens on the other. A substantial bridge carries North Parade Road over the river and then Isambard Kingdom Brunel's Great Western Railway spans the water before the site of Dolmead Wharf is reached beside the entrance to the canal. In the 18th century much of the stone used in the construction of Bath's classical thoroughfares came down by tramway to this point. A good deal of it was despatched along the Avon for export via Bristol to points as far afield as Dublin.

Halfpenny Footbridge tragically collapsed in 1877, overloaded by crowds on their way to the Bath & West Show, considerable loss of life ensued. The railway crosses the river a second time before Churchill Bridge is encountered, a rather bland modern replacement for Bath Old Bridge, an attractive three-arched structure of mid eighteenth century origin. The warehouses on the south bank which follow are a reminder of lost river trade. You may moor opposite and imagine you've arrived with a cargo of grain ex Avonmouth.

Around the next bend come memories of one of Britain's best loved railways, the incomparable Somerset & Dorset system, which ran out of Bath's Green Park station across the Mendip Hills to Bournemouth. This gracious terminus, whose booking hall might easily be mistaken for an elegant town house, witnessed its last trains depart in a flurry of steam in 1966, but has survived more or less intact to become part of an indoor market and a Sainsbury's supermarket - one does not know whether to laugh or to weep. Old photographs depicting the Pines Express storming up the 1 in 50 to Combe Down's suffocatingly confined tunnel, invariably expose a backdrop of gasholders which survive, incongruous now amidst retail parks and other 21st century paraphernalia. Gas tar was loaded on to barges for conveyance to Bristol until as comparatively recently as 1967. Two suspension bridges add dignity and interest to the scene.

The Keynote & Avon Canal

Bath Bottom Lock is numbered 7th in the sequence from Bristol. Numbers 8 and 9 were combined when the canal was restored at this point in 1976. The new chamber has an intimidating depth of 19ft 5ins, those inclined to claustrophobia and/or vertigo are advised to watch proceedings from a safe distance. Succeeding locks ascend the hillside in an agreeable manner, several of them sport ornamented iron footbridges at their tails cast locally by Stothert & Pitt in their riverside foundry. Abbey View Lock fulfils its obligations. Just above it you may pause temporarily to take on water or dispose of refuse, momentarily making the most of the intoxicating view.

Bath Top Lock marks the beginning of a lengthy pound which would be half as much again longer were it not for the solitary lock at Bradford, ten miles away. A useful boatyard and hire base follows before the canal romantically skirts the periphery of Sydney Gardens, encountering two tunnels and two elegant iron footbridges dated 1800. Cleveland House Tunnel is 173 feet long and the towpath runs through it. Above stands Cleveland House, former headquarters of the Kennet & Avon Canal Company. A trap-door in the tunnel roof was employed for facilitating the exchange of paperwork between clerks above and bargees below.

Sydney Gardens were opened as a 'resort of pleasure' in 1795, they were provided with an hotel, a bowling green and a labyrinth. The canal builders had to pay handsomely to invade the gardens' serenity. Thirty years later that calm was disturbed again by the passage of the London to

Bristol railway. At 165 yards, Sydney Gardens Tunnel is slightly shorter than its neighbour. Emerging from its eastern portal the canal runs shelf-like above the Avon Valley, shaking off the suburbs and sensing open countryside. Bridge 185 is a footbridge which replaced a swingbridge called Folly after a nearby pub destroyed during a Second World War bombing raid. The main London and Bristol railway line runs invisibly below, though passing trains break the silence, not, however, as intrusively as the relatively new stretch of A4 dual carriageway, confirmation that each new era of transport is more destructive than the last.

Essaying the easiest route around the hem of Bathampton Down, the canal continues to keep company with the River Avon, journeying on an almost north-south axis between Bathampton itself and Claverton. The scenery is delicious, and decidedly 'West Country' in feel, not something the canal network is necessarily well-aquainted with. A tramway was employed to bring stone down to Hampton Quarry Wharf by Bridge 182 when the canal was being built.

Claverton Pump was built to bring water up from the Avon to fill the canal. It was the work of John Rennie and its two water-wheels first began operating in 1813. It worked manfully for barely less than a century and a half before being replaced by a diesel pump. In 1976, however, it was lovingly restored by the Kennet & Avon Canal Trust. Whilst electric pumps do most of the work nowadays, the water-wheels perform their ancient rites on special days to an admiring public.

Bath *(Map 4)*

One doesn't need Unesco's 'World Heritage Site' seal of approval to facilitate the savouring of Bath's cohesive loveliness. By any criteria, this is one of Europe's most beautiful cities, and since one hasn't been able for almost forty years to arrive by steam train at the Queen Square (latterly Green Park) terminus of the Midland Railway, the Kennet & Avon Canal offers a consolatory alternative for visitors whose senses are fine-tuned to the more lofty ramifications of travel. The Roman Baths illustrate how far Bath's civilisation goes back, but it was the 18th century Welshman Beau Nash who galvanised the city's fame as a watering hole with few rivals. As Master of Ceremonies, he was the Tourism Development Officer of his era, and his grasp of publicity brought Society's crowds flocking to Bath as much for the social scene as for the quality of the waters. If Nash was Bath's best publicist, the architects John Wood, father and son, were the men most responsible for the city's inherent beauty and there is no way you should leave before

inspecting the extraordinary Royal Crescent, the Pump Room or Pulteney Bridge, let alone the 15th century Abbey and the Baths themselves. Make the most of it!

GREEN PARK BRASSERIE - Tel: 01225 338565. Bistro type restaurant housed in former station building, eat heartily then catch the ghost train to Evercreech Junction or wait for the live jazz Wed-Sat evenings.

STAR INN - The Vineyards. Listed amongst CAMRA's 'classics' for serious drinkers. Locally produced Abbey Ales on tap. No artificial noise but no food either. Tel: 01225 425072.

BROWNS - Orange Grove. Lively restaurant/bar. Tel: 01225 461199.

BISTRO PAPILLON - Margaret's Buildings (between The Circus and the Royal Crescent). Provencal cuisine. Tel: 01225 310064.

SALLY LUNN'S - North Parade Passage. Touristy but fun: "award-wining dinner at the oldest house in Bath". Tel: 01225 461634.

TILLEY'S BISTRO - North Parade Passage. Tel:

01225 484200. Les Routiers recommended French restaurant.

THE DOLPHIN - waterside, Weston Cut. Tel: 01225 445048. Friendly local offering bar meals, families made welcome, moorings adjacent.

Avoid the city centre chain stores and you'll be well rewarded. The GUILDHALL MARKET is a good starting point, it's located between the High Street and Pulteney Bridge. GREEN PARK MARKET is housed in the gracious environment of the old Midland Railway terminus. Arts and crafts feature Wednesday to Saturday, and there are farmers markets on selected Saturdays as well. Nearby it's feasible to moor on the Avon and stock up the galley at SAINSBURY'S. Collectors of antiquarian books will have to be kept on a tight leash, a leaflet available from the TIC currently lists about ten dealers, many located in Margaret's Buildings off Brock Street, not least Patterson Liddle (Tel: 01225 426722) who specialise in canals and railways.

continued on page 17

Pulteney Bridge, River Avon, Bath

Cleveland House at Bath, Kennet & Avon Canal

Michael Pearson

Lock No.11 at Bath, Kennet & Avon Canal

Michael Pearson

continued from page 14

ⓘ TOURIST INFORMATION - Abbey
Churchyard. Tel: 01225 477101.
GUIDE FRIDAY - open top bus tours of Bath and
its environs. Office at the railway station. Tel: 01225
444102.
THE ROMAN BATHS & PUMP ROOM - Abbey
Churchyard. Tel: 01225 477785.
JANE AUSTEN CENTRE - Gay Street. Tel: 01225
443000. Bath was the setting for *Northanger
Abbey* and *Persuasion* and their authoress lived
in the city from 1801 to 1806.
INDUSTRIAL HERITAGE CENTRE - Julian Road.
Tel: 01225 318348. A fascinating antidote to Bath's
(understandable) tendency to 18th century overkill.
WILLIAM HERSCHEL MUSEUM - New King
Street. Tel: 01225 311342. Small museum in
former home of famous astronomer.
NO.1 ROYAL CRESCENT - Tel: 01225 428126.
HOLBURNE MUSEUM - Tel: 01225 466669. Art
gallery located by Sydney Gardens within easy
reach of the canal before/after tackling all those
locks.
BATH BOATING STATION - Forester Road. Tel:
01225 466407.
MUSEUM OF COSTUME - Assembly Rooms.
Tel: 01225 477789. Fashion through the ages.

🚌 BUSES - Tel: 01225 477681.
TRAINS - Tel: 08457 484950. Useful links
with Bradford-on-Avon, Keynsham and Bristol for
towpath walkers and cyclists.
CYCLE HIRE - Avon Valley Cyclery. Tel: 01225
442442. Premises beneath Bristol bound platform
of the railway station by Halfpenny Bridge.

Bathampton *(Map 4)*

Bathampton was, until 1983, the site of Harbutt's
plasterine factory, something that generations
of children had been thankful for since William
Harbutt invented the substance in 1897. The
canalside church will be of interest to Australian
boating parties for the first Governor of New South
Wales lies buried here whilst the interior features
a small Australian Chapel. There are views
eastwards to Brown's Folly, a hillside tower
constructed to provide employment following the
Napoleonic Wars.
🫖 THE GEORGE INN - canalside Bridge 183.
Tel: 01225 425079. Classic country inn
predating the canal and said to be haunted by
the loser of the last legally fought duel in England.

BATHAMPTON MILL - riverside (down from Bridge
183). Tel: 01225 469758. All day family
restaurant/pub.
📮 Post office stores adjacent to Bridge 183.
More shops on housing estate uphill.
🚌 BUSES - First Badgerline X5 and X6
services hourly to/from Bath and Bradford.
Tel: 01225 464446.

Claverton *(Map 4)*

CLAVERTON PUMPING STATION - canalside
Bridge 180 (walk down Ferry Lane and over the
railway level crossing. Tel: 01225 483001.
Generally open April to October on Weds, Suns
and Bank Holidays but only in operation on special
pumping days - see local notices or telephone
for further information. www.claverton.org. On no
account should this be missed if at all possible!
AMERICAN MUSEUM - Claverton Manor.
Substantial early 19th century mansion housing
fascinating displays of Americana. Tel: 01225
460503. Light refreshments available. Open Easter
to October afternoons but not usually Mondays
except during August and Bank Holidays
www.americanmuseum.org.

3½ hours to have

DUNDAS is the focal point of this section of the canal. Here the K&A met the Somersetshire Coal Canal, which was built to carry that particular commodity from the collieries located south of Bath. From Dundas it ran for two miles to Midford where it divided, one arm extending to Radstock and the other to Paulton. The Radstock Arm was never in water, being converted into a tramroad in 1815 but the Paulton Arm was in business from 1805 until the end of the century. Perhaps the SCC's main claim to fame was its ill-fated caisson lock, designed to overcome a steep gradient at Combe Hay. Large enough to accommodate a narrowboat and pulled up and down a water filled cistern by means of a rack and pinion, it was a complete failure, being replaced by an inclined plane and eventually by a conventional flight of locks. Today the entrance lock to the SCC has been restored along with the first quarter of a mile of the waterway, in use for private moorings under the auspices of the Bath & Dundas Canal Company.

But it is John Rennie's sublime aqueduct that is the centre of attention at Dundas. Rennie's reputation never quite matched that of Brindley or Telford, but he was the builder of several notable aqueducts, Avoncliff (further along the K&A) and Lune (on the Lancaster Canal) being two of his best. Arguably, though, it was Dundas that was his

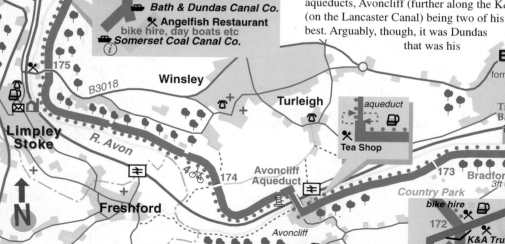

BRASSKNOCKER BASIN
🚢 **Bath & Dundas Canal Co.**
🍴 **Angelfish Restaurant**
bike hire, day boats etc
🚢 **Somerset Coal Canal Co.**
ⓘ

Winsley

Turleigh

Limpley Stoke

Freshford

Avoncliff Aqueduct

Avoncliff

aqueduct

Tea Shop

Country Park

bike hire

K&A Trust

Bradford-on-Avon
former mills **Town Centre**

Tithe Barn

Bradford Lock
3ft 6ins

Budgens

The Beehive

Beef & Barge

Bradford Marina/Sally Boats

B3109 to Frome

A363 to Trowbridge

Dundas Aqueduct, Kennet & Avon Canal

finest work. Completed in 1805 and named after Charles Dundas, the first chairman of the Kennet & Avon Canal Company, the 150-yard, three-arched aqueduct was built of Bath stone in the Doric style with a solid parapet featuring balustrading at each end, and cornices projecting some four feet from the parapet on both faces. At the beginning of 2003 a two-year, £1 million refurbishment programme commenced on this Grade 1 listed structure and special care is being taken to ensure that a colony of bats are not disturbed.

Crossing into Wiltshire, the canal glides through the delectable Limpley Stoke Valley seemingly without a care in the world. It wasn't always so, for the length between Limpley Stoke Bridge and Avoncliff Aqueduct became known as the 'dry section', so prone was it to leakage and landslips. The canal bed now has a layer of hardcore on a porous membrane, which is itself covered by a layer of polythene sheeting and a final bed of reinforced concrete.

A small community - pub, station, tearoom and cluster of houses - has grown up around Avoncliff Aqueduct. Similar to Dundas just down the valley, Avoncliff is a three-arched Bath stone structure, although there is evidence of extensive brick repair work, particularly to the eastern facade.

It also had a tramroad link to a local quarry, in this case the Upper Westwood Quarry to the south of the canal.

Bradford-on-Avon was where it all began as far as the Kennet & Avon Canal was concerned, the first sod being cut just outside the Canal Tavern in 1794. Reflect on the past - an army of unfortunate, ill educated navvies toiling laboriously away with picks and shovels by day, then drinking and brawling by night whilst you enjoy present day Bradford, one of the most picturesque ports of call on the entire K&A. There were once two wharves in this thriving wool town, one above and one below the lock. Upper Wharf is especially attractive with dry dock (formerly a gauging dock), wharfinger's house and pub, together with a K&A Canal Trust shop. Half a mile to the east, opposite Bradford Marina, the nineteenth century Beehive Inn stands close to the proposed junction with the intended Dorset & Somerset Canal, scheduled to run via Frome, Wincanton and Sturminster Newton to Shillingstone Okeford near Blandford Forum, with an arm from Frome to the Nettlebridge collieries. What a fantastic canal the D&S would have been, but although the enabling Act received Royal Assent in March 1796, work on the main line never actually began due to financial difficulties.

Monkton Combe *(Map 5)*

BRASSKNOCKER BASIN - an imaginative modern development at the junction of the Somerset Coal Canal. Attractions include the Angelfish Restaurant (Tel: 01225 723483); the Bath & Dundas Canal Co (Tel: 01225 722292) for day boat, canoe and cycle hire and the Somerset Coal Canal Company - see Boating Directory page 78. Refreshments are also available at the nearby Viaduct Hotel (Tel: 01225 723187). The Kennet & Avon Canal Trust operate boat trips from the basin aboard Jubilee. Tel: 01373 813957.

Limpley Stoke *(Map 5)*

Pretty riverside community a short walk downhill from Bridge 175. Facilities include a small post office stores, a nice pub called the Hop Pole (Tel: 01225 723134) and Nightingale's Restaurant which is open Tue-Sat evenings and Sun lunchtimes - Tel: 01225 723150. Look out for the old railway station (now a private home). The Camerton branch ran from here until the early 1950s and the much loved Ealing comedy *The Titfield Thunderbolt* was filmed on the line after it had been officially closed and some scenes were shot at the Hop Pole.

Avoncliff *(Map 5)*

Most canal users will be tempted to linger awhile at Avoncliff and savour the setting. Whilst most eyes will be drawn to the aqueduct, spare a moment to look at the tiny railway station, almost as pretty and as cared for as if it were on some preserved steam line. Refreshments can be obtained at the popular Cross Guns Inn (Tel: 01225 862335) or the Mad Hatter Tearooms.

Bradford-on-Avon (Map 5)

Teetering on the brink of its clifftop setting, mellow, medieval Bradford-on-Avon resembles a small version of Bath, and being smaller can be appreciated and assimilated all the more easily. Amongst many outstanding buildings you'll come upon a Saxon church, a tithe barn and a 14th century bridge with a chapel on it, though in less godly times this chapel saw use as a lock-up for miscreants. This lovely town's fortunes were built on wool and weaving and many of its buildings, both domestic and commercial, reflect the heyday of this lost industry.

LOCK INN CAFE - canalside below Bradford Lock. Wonderful establishment offering food, canoe and bike hire and good humour. Tel: 01225 868068. www.the lockinn.co.uk
CANAL TAVERN - canalside below Bradford Lock. Tel: 01225 867426. Wadworth ales and a wide range of food.
THE MAHARAJA - adjacent canal wharf. Indian tandoori restaurant/take-away. Tel: 01225 866424.
THE BARGE - canalside above Bradford Lock. Tel: 01225 863403.
THE BEEHIVE - canalside Bridge 170. Tel: 01225 863620. Nicely unspoilt, guest ales and bar meals; 'a beer-lover's dream' according to the GBG!
BEEF & BARGE - Bradford Marina. Tel: 01225 862004.
THE COTTAGE CO-OPERATIVE - Town centre. Organic cafe. Tel: 01225 867444.
THE DANDY LION - Market Place. Tel: 01225 863433. Lively town centre pub, good on food.
SWAN HOTEL - Market Place. Tel: 01225 868686. Comfortable hotel dating from 1500 offering bar and restaurant food.
Tearooms, fish & chips & Chinese too!

The town centre is ten minutes walk down from the canal and there are heaps of nice old-fashioned shops. We found two good delis - MAPLES and the CHEESE BOARD - and a small bookshop called EX LIBRIS. More prosaically, there's a BUDGENS supermarket by Bridge 171.
i TOURIST INFORMATION - Silver Street (adjacent to Town Bridge. Tel: 01225 865797.
BUSES - FirstBadgerline. Tel: 01225 464446.
TRAINS - connections for Bath via Avoncliff and Westbury via Trowbridge. Tel: 08457 484950.

Trowbridge (Map 6)

One suspects that few canal users make the effort to visit Trowbridge, the County Town of Wiltshire, upon which the cloying smell of Bowyers food processing plant hangs like a wet blanket. On foot it's a bleak trudge which takes the best part of half an hour. Buses from Hilperton alleviate such discomforts, but in truth Bradford or Devizes are better deserving of your curiosity, though here and there amongst the mediocrity are many handsome buildings in local stone which deserve a better setting. Even Ushers Brewery was in the process of being demolished at the time of our reconnaissance.

KINGS ARMS - Hilperton near Bridge 166. Tel: 01225 755168. Food, families welcome.
Full range of shops and banks in the town centre. Interesting indoor market. Lidl supermarket about ten minutes walk from Hilperton Wharf. The petrol station near Bridge 166 has a useful shop and cash machine.
i TOURIST INFORMATION - St Stephens Place. Tel: 01225 777054.
TRAINS - to/from Bath via Bradford. Tel: 08457 484950.

Semington (Map 6)

SOMERSET ARMS - 5 minutes walk south of Bridge 160. Tel: 01380 870067. Comfortable old coaching inn offering good bar and restaurant meals.
Dayboat hire from Tranquil Boats - see page 79.

Seend Cleeve (Map 7)

THE BARGE INN - canalside Bridge 154. Tel: 01380 828230. Very popular waterside pub. Wadworth beer and a wide range of food.
BREWERY INN - 5 minutes south from Bridge 154. Unspoilt village local. Tel: 01380 828463.

Seend (Map 7)

Gracious village somewhat compromised by traffic on the A361. Post office stores and pub.

Sells Green (Map 7)

THREE MAGPIES - north of Bridge 149. Tel: 01380 828389. Wadworths, bar and restaurant meals.

THE Kennet & Avon Canal skirts the urban periphery of Trowbridge. An Act was passed in 1769 to build a branch into the town but construction didn't ensue. Two modest, yet elegant aqueducts transport the canal over the River Biss, a tributary of the Avon, and the Westbury-Bath railway line respectively. The single arched Biss Aqueduct, whilst never soaring to the same heights (literally or metaphorically) as Dundas and Avoncliff further west, is especially handsome. And then there are the remains - admittedly scant - of two wharves beside Hilperton Road Bridge, Marsh Wharf and Hilperton Wharf both being built to serve Trowbridge in the absence of that branch. To the north is the Nestle factory at Staverton, occupying the site of a former clothing mill, once a major employer in this erstwhile important weaving area.

It's difficult to visualise sleepy Semington as a busy canal junction but such was the case in the early part of the nineteenth century. The Wilts & Berks Canal, opened in 1810, ran from here for 51 heavily locked miles to the Thames at Abingdon (see Map 27) via Melksham, Swindon and Challow. Its commercial success was short-lived, however, competition from the GWR railway from London to Bristol bringing about its downfall. Through traffic became impossible following the collapse of an aqueduct between Chippenham and Calne in 1901. Little evidence of the junction remains, except for the toll collector's house, now in private ownership, the old stop lock being hidden under the obviously keen gardener's immaculate collection of sweet peas, lavender and hollyhocks. A Wilks & Berks Canal Trust was formed in 1997 with the long term aim of restoring the canal to navigation. An associate Amenity Group can be contacted on 01628 544666.

The two locks at Semington mark the end of a five mile level pound from Bradford-on-Avon, and they are quickly followed by a flight of five at Seend.

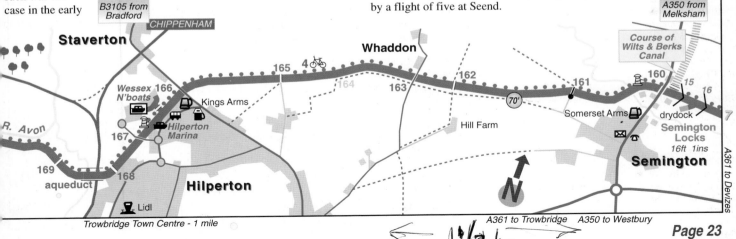

HOW green and lush is the countryside around Seend Cleeve. Swing bridges abound, and there's a flight of five locks too, giving you extra time to appreciate the soft rolling hills that characterise this part of Wiltshire. The Barge Inn, situated below the middle lock of the flight, is one of the most popular pubs on the entire K&A and stands on the site of Seend Wharf. Dating back to 1805, The Barge comprises the former wharf house and stables and was once owned by the Duke of Somerset's family. In 1916 it became the home of the 'Wiltshire Giant' Fred Kempster (8 feet 2 inches) whose brother-in-law was the landlord.

A field to the east of the Barge was the site of a most unlikely industry in the nineteenth century, ironstone having been discovered on Seend Hill. Two blast furnaces were built, together with tramway connections to the canal and a branch railway to Devizes, but the enterprise was never a financial success. Nevertheless, mining of iron ore continued until after the First World War. The lines of the two tramways are still discernible, whilst the elaborate house of the iron master is visible on the hillside above the canal.

Distant views of Salisbury Plain, some twenty miles away to the south, present themselves as the canal drifts across Summerham Brook on a small aqueduct. Ever mindful of maximising water supply, the K&A utilises water from the brook which is channelled into the waterway via the Seend Feeder.

Lots of people seem to like mooring overnight between bridges 149 and 152. The countryside is blissful and paths radiate from the swing-bridges for the exercising of dogs. In doing so one might come upon the melancholy trackbed of an old railway which once linked Devizes with the outside world. Later, as the light fades, the campanologists of Seend may lull you to sleep.

Bridge 148 marks the site of Wragg's Wharf from which a family of that name once plied with a pair of boats to and from Dunkerton Colliery on the Somerset Coal Canal. Commercial trade on the Kennet & Avon petered out under Great Western Railway ownership, not surprisingly the railway company promoted trains at the expense of boats and by and large the local economies were happy to comply.

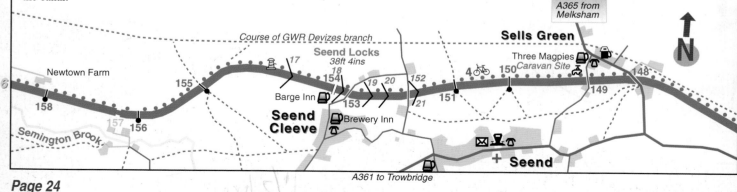

Misty morning at Seend, Kennet & Avon Canal

Locking down Devizes Locks, Kennet & Avon Canal

DEVIZES Locks were the last major engineering works to be completed before the canal's opening in 1810, and one of the final restoration projects to be finished prior to reopening in 1990. The locks exert a powerful influence on the waterway to this day, with cruising itineraries being carefully planned around their intimidating presence.

But first some facts and figures. One of the 'Seven Wonders of the Waterways' as selected by Robert Aickman, the Devizes flight of 29 widebeam locks raises (or lowers) the level of the canal by 237 feet in just over two miles. They come in three groups: seven at Foxhangers, sixteen at Caen Hill and six at the town end of the flight. Whilst the locks were under construction in the early 1800s a tramroad provided a link between Foxhangers and Devizes, as evidenced by the towpath arches in the road bridges that cross the canal. The locks were built of brick, supplied by the now disused brickworks beside the Caen Hill section. To address serious water supply problems, a back pumping station was installed at Foxhangers in 1996, capable of returning 32 million litres of water per day to the top of the flight - equivalent to one lockful every eleven minutes.

Impressive though the entire Devizes flight may be, it is the Caen Hill section that wins all the plaudits - and deservedly so. Named after the home town of a group of French prisoners of war who were made to work here during the construction of the flight, the sixteen closely spaced Caen Hill locks make light work of a 1 in 30 gradient. Each lock is equipped with an extensive side pond, virtually a small reservoir, designed by John Rennie to guarantee an adequate water supply.

But how does it feel to arrive at the foot (or top) of the flight with all those locks ahead of you? Well you certainly won't be doing much else that day, five to six hours being considered a good performance for clearance of the flight. But don't be intimidated, for the locks are well maintained and relatively easy to operate, and, in high season at least,

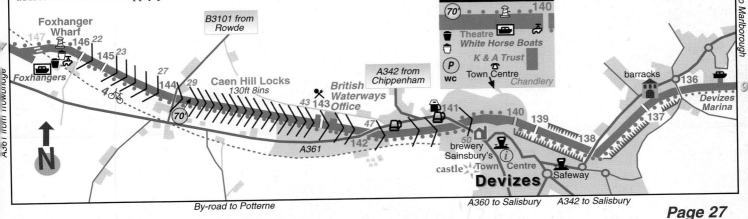

you'll probably have other boaters to share the work with you. Settle in to a rhythm, relax and enjoy every moment of one of the best experiences the waterway system has to offer. The surroundings can only add to your enjoyment, being pleasantly pastoral with splendid views down the flight to the Avon Valley.

Devizes once possessed three wharves, Sussex, Lower and Town, of which only the latter survives. Built around 1812, its early trade was in coal from the Somersetshire Coal Canal, later traffic bringing in agricultural goods, brick, stone and timber; plus, of course, raw materials and finished products heading to and from Wadworth's brewery, situated less than a yard of ale's distance from the canal. Today two admirably restored buildings stand proudly on the wharf: a former warehouse now serves as the Wharf Theatre, whilst an erstwhile granary and wine store is now the headquarters of the Kennet & Avon Canal Trust. With a small hire fleet and trip boat also based here, the wharf buzzes with activity on summer weekends and is an excellent place to recuperate from (or gird your loins for) the rigours of the Devizes Locks.

Devizes *(Map 8)*

The Kennet & Avon is more fortunate than most canals when one considers the appeal of the towns it serves. Devizes is no exception - some might argue the best of them all. An ancient Wiltshire market town, it is widely known in beer-drinking circles for the excellence of the ale brewed by Wadworth, from whose red brick works a horse and dray still makes local deliveries about the town. David Verey's 1956 *Shell Guide to Wiltshire* spoke enthusiastically of the 'restrained dignity of its streets, the red brick Georgian houses contrasting with ashlar-faced public buildings in the Bath manner and the fine proportions of its market place'. Within the precincts of this market place we sheltered in a doorway from the rain devouring fish & chips from grease-proof (but not waterproof) wrapping and watched the cream of Wiltshire society going about their daily existence, a rewarding experience in more ways than one.

THE CASTLE HOTEL - New Park Street. CTC and Les Routiers recommended hotel offering cosy public rooms and bar/restaurant meals. Tel: 01380 729300.

WHARFSIDE RESTAURANT - canalside eating place offering farmhouse style lunches and light meals. Tel: 01380 726051.

LOCK COTTAGE TEA ROOM - canalside by Lock 44. Tel: 01380 724880.

THE ARTICHOKE - Bath Road (by Bridge 141). Wadworth local within view of brewery. Beer delivered by horse! Tel: 01380 723400.

BLACK HORSE - adjacent canal by Bridge 142/Lock 47. Tel: 01380 723930.

BEAR HOTEL - Market Place. Tel: 01380 722444. Bar and restaurant meals. Dates from 1599, the portrait artist Sir Thomas Lawrence lived here as a boy.

LEES FISH & CHIPS - Monday Market Street. Open lunch and evenings daily ex Sundays.

Shopping is fun in Devizes. Access from the Wharf is via Couch Lane and Snuff Street, beyond which the Market Place opens up in all its glory. On High Street you'll find the CONTINENTAL DELICATESSEN and COOK & SONS the butchers. Another good butcher is WALTER ROSE on Sidmouth Street who also deals in fish. DEVIZES BOOKSHOP is located in Handel House on Sidmouth Street. The COVERED MARKET is a lovely building in its own right: on Tuesdays it plays host to an antiques market, whilst on Thursdays, Fridays and Saturdays commerce is of a more general nature. Should you need any accessories for your boat then try the WHARFSIDE CHANDLERY - Tel: 01380 725007.

DEVIZES VISITOR CENTRE - Market Place. Tel: 01380 729408. Tourist Information Centre plus displays delving into the town's colourful medieval heyday.

CANAL TRUST CENTRE - Devizes Wharf. Tel: 01380 729489. Excellent shop and museum operated by the Kennet & Avon Canal Trust.

DEVIZES MUSEUM - Long Street. Tel: 01380 727369. The history of Wiltshire and Devizes in particular.

WADWORTH SHIRES - Northgate. Open Monday to Friday 13.30 to 15.30. Wadworth's keep four Shire horses to make deliveries within a two mile radius of the town. Two horses haul each dray and each dray can carry up to three tons of beer.

BUSES - Wiltshire Bus Line - Tel: 08457 090899 National Traveline - Tel: 0870 608 2 608.

Hotel boats on the Kennet & Avon near All Cannings

The Wiltshire Downs - Kennet & Avon Canal near Picked Hill.

SCUDDING clouds cast energetic shadows on the sculptured downs as the canal's dreamlike and curvaceous traverse of the Vale of Pewsey is punctuated by remote villages, for the most part now bereft of shops and pubs. The widespread use of brick surprises, outnumbering stone and thatch until you see pockets of chalk exposed on the downs and realise that it would not be an ideal building material.

Only the most time-constrained canal traveller will be able to resist a detour up on to the tumuli littered top of the downs, scaling the chalky escarpment to where the Wansdyke once delineated prehistoric territories. These Marlborough Downs form the highest part of Wiltshire, just falling short of a thousand feet above sea level. On a clear day, the locals say, you can see the spire of Salisbury Cathedral peeping out above its own plain to the south.

Hereabouts are the headwaters of another River Avon, not to be confused with the one in the title of the Kennet & Avon Canal. This Avon flows south off these chalky uplands, receives encouragement from the Wylye, the Nadder and the Bourne, and eventually reaches its inevitable appointment with the English Channel at Christchurch in Dorset.

This is the Long Pound, and it lives up to its name, consisting of fifteen restful, lock-less miles with only the odd swing bridge to disturb a boater's reverie. Time, perhaps, to picture yourself the captain of a widebeam, horse-drawn barge, Pewsey bound with grain from Bristol docks.

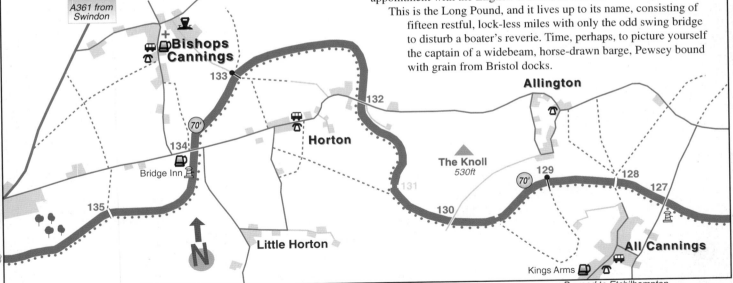

A361 from Swindon

Bishops Cannings

133

132

Allington

70'

Horton

134

Bridge Inn

The Knoll
530ft

129

128

70'

127

135

130

131

10

N

Little Horton

All Cannings

Kings Arms

By-road to Coate

By-road to Etchilhampton

*T*HE famous Alton Barnes White Horse is readily visible from the canal to the north in the vicinity of Honey Street. It was cut in 1812, though not without some delay after the original contractor decamped with the money.

Overlooked by a high, red brick chimney, Honey Street Wharf was owned by Robbins, Lane & Pinniger, the last regular commercial users of the canal between Avonmouth and Hungerford. Their barge *Unity* carried softwood from Avonmouth and timber from Hungerford to the Honey Street Wharf sawmill. The company also built many of the boats used on the K&A, Basingstoke Canal and River Wey prior to leaving the site in the late 1940s. Nowadays a timber yard and agricultural merchant provide Honey Street with at least some semblance of commercial activity. With tourist eyes we may object to such environmental intrusion, but at least it reminds us why the canal was built in the first place.

Most imposing is the Barge Inn, not to be confused for a rendezvous with the one at Seend (Map 7). In earlier times it played an even more significant role in the life of Honey Street Wharf, being an important stabling point for boat horses, a bakery, a brewery and a slaughterhouse all rolled into one. Following a destructive fire in 1858, it was completely rebuilt within six months, testimony to its importance to canal trade and commerce.

The hills close in - Woodborough and Pecked being less than half a mile from the canal - as you drift languidly past Wilcot, well known for its 'Wide Water' and its 'Ladies Bridge'. In an echo of events at Tixall Wide on the Trent & Mersey Canal, the K&A engineers collided with the intransigence of Lady Susannah Wroughton, who insisted that the canal cut through her grounds had to be in the guise of an ornamental lake. Ladies Bridge at the western end of the Wide was a similar gesture of appeasement to the gentility, the bridge being decorated with ornamental stonework and equipped with balustraded parapets.

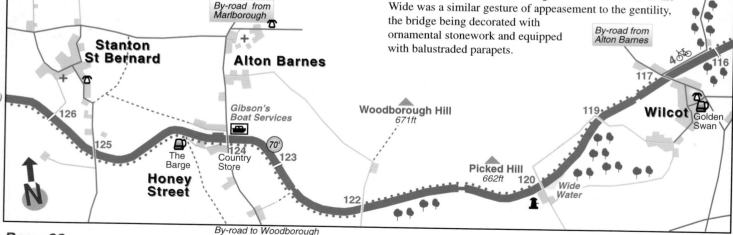

FIRMLY ensconced in the Vale of Pewsey, the canal skirts the lush grounds of Stowell Park complete with its classical mansion. Elegant Stowell Park Suspension Bridge, carrying a private footpath into the park, is of unusual construction, being made from jointed iron bars instead of the more usual platform hung on wire cable.

A deep tree lined cutting leads on to Pewsey Wharf. The town itself lies half a mile away down the A345, but a small settlement - comprising cottages, pub, shop and tearoom - appears to be thriving beside the canal. Overlooked by 900 foot Martinsell Hill, the canal wends its lockless way through the Vale of Pewsey, undisturbed in its peaceful slumbers. However, if you're eastbound, prepare to meet the main London-Plymouth railway line, which comes close alongside hereabouts and is to become your almost constant companion for the remainder of the journey to Reading.

The Great Western Railway was unkind to the Kennet & Avon Canal. It bought it out in 1852 and allowed it to languish, though theoretically it remained open to navigation until Nationalisation in 1948, following which the British Transport Commission proposed its abandonment. Yet how compatible are rail and canal routes, how unobtrusively both blend into and complement the surrounding countryside - contrast the six-lane monstrosity that is the M4, not more than twenty miles away to the north. For us there is nothing more reassuring than mooring close by a railway, passing trains providing a comforting backdrop, not least in the wee small hours of the morning when man's sense of insecurity reaches its zenith.

Speaking of zeniths, the K&A reaches its own summit at Wootton Rivers, where a flight of four locks raises the level by 32 feet to the heady heights of 450 feet above sea level. Having fallen into a state of disrepair in the Fifties, the locks were reopened in June 1973.

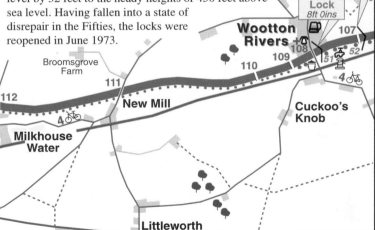

Pewsey *(Map 11)*

Focus of its fecund vale, and high on feel-good factor, Pewsey admirably repays the trouble taken to walk down from the wharf, though those less energetically predisposed can call from The Waterfront cafe for a taxi or Wigglybus. Personally, we feel that after a long stint at the tiller, the walk can only be good for you. At the time of our visit the pleasing aroma of woodsmoke hung over the little town. Passing under the railway (whose station is beautifully appointed) one comes at length to Marshall's Bakery, the first welcome outlier of civilisation. Further reassuring signs include the Post Office and a space for Tuesday's little market. A weatherbeaten statue depicting King Alfred (but erected to show local approval of the crowning of King George V) marks the right-angled commencement of High Street which crosses a pretty stream with a sandy bed, no less than the 'Hampshire' Avon.

THE WATERFRONT - canalside, Pewsey Wharf. Tel: 01672 564020. Licensed cafe/restaurant: lively, informal, eccentric and serving anything from a bacon sandwich to a steak.

THE FRENCH HORN - adjacent Bridge 114. Charming little brick built pub just north of the wharf, said to have gained its name from the use of a horn to summon French prisoners of war at work on the canal. Food, families welcome. Tel: 01672 562443.

SHANTY - High Street. Tandoori takeaway. Tel: 01672 564640.

DAYTIME BITES - High Street. Amiable little coffee shop. Tel: 01672 564004.

The Boatman's Locker (Tel: 01672 564700) at Pewsey Wharf stocks a small but handy selection of essential groceries as well as gifts and souvenirs. The town itself is presided over by a sizeable Co-op supermarket. There is also a Lloyds TSB bank (with cash machine), a newsagent and a pharmacy, but try as we might we couldn't locate a butcher.

BUSES - regular services run to Swindon and Salisbury, the latter worthy of an excursion perhaps. Tel: 01722 336855. The Wigglybus will help you with towpath instalments - Tel: 01249 460600.

TRAINS - First Great Western services to/from London Paddington with connections at Westbury for Trowbridge, Bradford and Bath. Tel: 08457 484950.

Wootton Rivers *(Map 11)*

Idyllic canalside village with a most curious clock in its church and an excellent inn called the ROYAL OAK (Tel: 01672 810332) delightfully constructed of weatherboarding and thatch and advertising itself as a venue for civil weddings- though most in our experience have a tendency towards being decidedly uncivil.

Wilcot *(Map 10)*

A peaceful village with lots of thatch in evidence grouped about a sizeable green curiously sporting just one set of goalposts. The GOLDEN SWAN is a nice Wadworth pub - Tel: 01672 562289. Food and accommodation.

Honey Street *(Map 10)*

THE BARGE INN - canalside. Tel: 01672 851705. Atmospheric and historic canal pub offering a wide selection of food, a popular gathering point for crop-circle investigators.

Bishops Cannings *(Map 9)*

Home of the original Moonrakers who claimed that they were idiotically attempting to rake the moon (for its cheese) from a pond when ambushed by an Exciseman who (rightly) suspected them of retrieving smuggled brandy from a pond. The explanation is said to have worked! On another famous occasion the whole population of the village is reputed to have walked to Devizes to see a comet pass through the heavens. James I was entertained by the vicar here early in the 17th century. The spired church is especially imposing and contains some fine lancet windows and a curious ancient chair with Latin inscriptions. Facilities include a post office stores and a Wadworth pub called the CROWN INN (Tel: 01380 860218) which does food and welcomes families.

Horton *(Map 9)*

BRIDGE INN - canalside Bridge 134. Tel: 01380 860273. Convivial Wadworth pub offering food and good moorings for an overnight stop.

All Cannings *(Map 9)*

A peaceful village with good visitor moorings recently shorn of its shop but retaining an excellent pub - the KINGS ARMS (Tel: 01380 860328) and a bus service called the Wiltshire Wigglybus which will pick you up to order by telephoning 01249 460600 and whisk you away to the fleshpots of Devizes and or Pewsey.

SOMEONE ought to write a book about canal summits: their generic traits, their inherent variety. Not only did the 18th century engineers have to climb, when they got to the top they had to find water. The Kennet & Avon's two mile summit does not present too many opportunities for water storage and is obviously hardly long enough to act as a linear reservoir. The solution came from Wilton Water, a small reservoir fed by springs, and a pair of pumping engines were provided to feed the summit. Two centuries later, little has changed other than provision of new electric pumps and preservation of the old steam monsters who originally did the work, more of which in a moment.

Meanwhile consider the summit itself. Burbage Wharf was built in the nineteenth century to handle trade from Marlborough, which never received its promised branch canal. The wharf's present wooden crane is a replica of the original which stood there until 1972; in its heyday it handled copious quantities of timber, stone, coal and agricultural produce. Adjacent Burbage Bridge, carrying the busy A338 Marlborough-Andover road, is an early example of a skew bridge, ie one that crosses the canal at an angle rather than at ninety degrees. John Rennie is thought to have been the first canal engineer to master the skew technique and further K&A examples include Beech Grove Bridge (No 98) at Crofton and Mill Bridge (No 97) at Great Bedwyn. The railway also had a goods facility at Burbage which had originally been conceived as an interchange point between the two transport modes. Once, however, the railway had provided a branch line to Marlborough use of the siding settled down to spasmodic cattle trains run in connection with Marlborough's famous cattle fairs. There were *two* railway lines linking Savernake with Marlborough, a Great Western branch which terminated in the town and the celebrated Midland & South Western Railway, a cross country route linking Southampton with Cheltenham.

Skirting the periphery of Savernake Forest - 2,300 acres of mixed woodland

course of Great Western Railway

course of Midland & South-Western Railway

A346 from Marlborough

site of Savernake High Level station

By-road from Savernake Forest

Burbage Wharf 104

BRUCE TUNNEL 502 yards

Crofton

Crofton Pump

Crofton Locks 61ft 0ins

Roman

13

100

61

60

Walk to Windmill

70'

4

SUMMIT 450ft

site of Savernake Low Level station

59

Wilton Water

tumuli

105

54 Wootton Top Lock 8ft 0ins

Ram Alley

106

53

Brimslade Lock 8ft 0ins

103

55 102 56

57

58 101

70'

N

Stibb Green

criss-crossed by a network of paths - the canal dives headlong into Bruce Tunnel, named after Thomas Bruce, the Earl of Ailesbury, who owned much of the land in the vicinity. It was perhaps ironic that the Kennet & Avon Canal Company should name the tunnel thus, for it was only on the good Earl's insistence that it had to be built at all. A deep cutting - like those on either side - would doubtless have coped with the low hill standing in the canal's way. At 502 yards long and wide enough for two narrowboats to pass inside, it's the only one worthy of the name on the entire K&A, and has no towpath, working boatmen pulling their craft through by chains fixed to the wall whilst their horses crossed above. Pedestrians still use the old horse path, of course, and, as is so often the case, are treated to much that the boater misses. The former Savernake Forest Hotel for example, and the remains of the two railway stations, and they alone can witness the railway's sleight of hand in crossing to the opposite bank of the canal while it passes unknowingly through its tunnel.

All too quickly, the summit level is done with. Observe the feeder channel from Wilton Water and the remains of the bridge carrying the lines of the Midland & South Western Junction Railway across the canal as you approach the Crofton flight. Here nine locks drop you down by some 61 feet amidst the gently rolling hills that have become the canal's trademark. Crofton Pumping Station is famous enough to require little introduction, being one of the Kennet & Avon's 'must see' highlights. Initial proposals were for a lower and longer (eighteen-mile) summit level with a 4,300 yard tunnel extending almost to Wootton Rivers, but these were amended on the advice of William Jessop, which was readily accepted by John Rennie; hence the need for pumps to raise water from Wilton Water up forty feet to the higher summit. Two steam engines manfully did the job until 1959 when the removal of the top twenty feet of the pumphouse chimney resulted in insufficient draught for the boilers and they were replaced by first a diesel pump and then an electric one. The Crofton Society subsequently restored the steam pumps and the building, which was officially reopened by Sir John Betjeman in August 1970; regular 'steam weekends' have been held ever since.

Stibb Green (Map 12)

Outlying part of Burbage approximately half a mile's walk from Bruce Tunnel. Bus connections to Marlborough (Tel: 01722 336855) and a nice pub called the THREE HORSESHOES - Tel: 01672 810324.

Savernake Forest (Map 12)

Savernake was a royal hunting forest and is mentioned in the Doomsday Book. The Grand Avenue of beech trees was planted by Capability Brown two hundred and fifty years ago. Less than a mile north of the canal stands the Ailesbury Column erected to give thanks for the recovery of George III from madness.

Crofton (Map 12)

Crofton Pumping Station houses two Cornish beam engines, the oldest built by Boulton & Watt dating from 1812, its junior a Harvey's of Hayle engine of 1845. Steam is raised through a hand-stoked, coal fired Lancashire boiler. Between them, the two engines can lift two tons of water to the summit at every stoke. Wilton Water was enlarged into a reservoir in 1836 and has become rich in birdlife. The pumping station is open to the public daily from Easter to October, whilst the machinery itself comes to life on selected weekends - Tel: 01672 870300 for further information. An old Roman Road makes up part of a charming circular walk of just over an hour's duration based on Crofton. The Venta Belgarum once linked Winchester with Mildenhall near Marlborough, now it will take you from the canal to Wilton Windmill which operates on Sunday and Bank Holiday Monday afternoons between Easter and the end of September - Tel: 01672 870427. Ironically, the mill had to be built in 1821 because the canal was taking too much water out of the River Bedwyn for local water mills to be driven. The windmill remained in everyday use until 1920. Restoration commenced in 1976. Nowadays it is floodlit from dusk until 10pm. For the sake of variety you can return along a footpath bordering Wilton Water, suitably refreshed, perhaps, following a visit to The Swan pub in Wilton village.

THIS is a classic section of the Kennet & Avon, much frequented by photographers and artists anxious to capture images of the canal in its parallel proximity to the Great Western main line. You might argue that the railway's cast list lacks variety nowadays - it would have been nice to have been here when 'Kings' were still entrusted to the *Cornish Riviera Express* (or even 'Westerns' or 'Warships') - but there is still a thrill to be experienced as the canal traveller is overtaken by one of the ubiquitous High Speed Trains or, better still, by one of the lengthy stone trains.

The Battle of Bedwyn was fought here in 675 between Escuin, a Wessex nobleman who had seized the throne of Queen Saxburga, and the redoubtable King Wulfhere of Mercia. The fighting was fierce and the loss of life substantial before Escuin forced King Wulfhere to retreat northwards. The battle to restore this section of the Kennet & Avon Canal was far less bloody and ended with all the locks between Crofton and Hungerford being reopened by 1988.

Great Bedwyn Wharf, home to a small boatyard and base for a charitable trip boat, is unusual in that it was built on the towpath side. Whilst never handling as much trade as Burbage Wharf, three miles to the west, it once accommodated two coal merchants and was still shipping wheat to Aldermaston until just before the First World War.

Burnt Mill Lock was originally called Knight's Mill Lock, gaining its new name after Great Bedwyn water mill was destroyed by fire early in the 19th century. Two hundred years on, one mischievously wonders if it was 'an insurance job' following the reduction in flow associated with the advent of the canal. However, the infant River Dun certainly adds to the scene as the canal proceeds past Little Bedwyn which is where all the photographers like to gather. If they are out in numbers, their presence may well indicate the imminent appearance of a steam-hauled special.

The lazy, lockless miles of the Long Pound are but a distant memory now as the locks come along thick and fast. But there's a delightful timelessness about this little known corner of East Wiltshire that puts you in no mood to hurry.

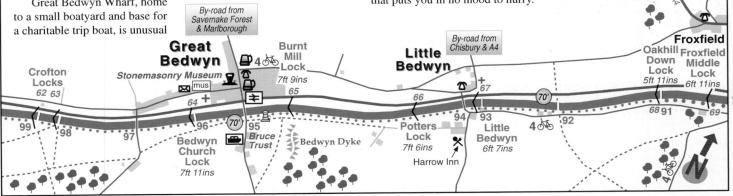

A Paddington bound express crosses the Kennet & Avon Canal below Picketfield Lock near Hungerford

David Alison

Great Bedwyn (Map 13)

The name Bedwyn is believed to have derived from 'Bedwind' or 'Bedwine', an old English word referring to a place where clematis grows in great profusion. One senses Great Bedwyn was a more important place in the past, at one time it returned two Members of Parliament! Nowadays it lies at the western edge of London's commuter belt - Thames Trains' outer suburban service terminates here!

CROSS KEYS - village centre. Tel: 01672 870678. Lively village local.

THREE TUNS - village centre. Tel: 01672 870280.

Village stores open daily 7am-8pm except for Sundays when it closes at 1pm. The Post Office adjoins Lloyds stonemasonry workshop (Tel: 01672 870234) which features an astonishing collection of monuments.

BUSES - frequent Mon-Sat link with Marlborough. Tel: 08457 090 899.

TRAINS - Thames Trains provide a useful local service running to/from London Paddington providing incremental succour for towpath walkers. Tel: 08457 484950.

Little Bedwyn (Map 13)

St Michael's Church is built of local flint and completes a charming scene. The HARROW INN (Tel: 01672 870871) is a sophisticated restaurant and bar as opposed to a village local. "No draught beer and no bar snacks" but a mouthwatering menu none the less.

Hungerford (Map 14)

Hungerford's broad, sloping High Street strides confidently down to the canal, concealing the fact that the town is comparatively small. Nevertheless, it comes alive at least once a year on the occasion of the 'Hocktide Ceremony' (held on the second Tuesday following Easter) whereupon ninety-nine commoners are summoned to the Town Hall by the blowing of a horn. Two 'Tuttimen' are elected and proceed from house to house exchanging oranges for kisses. All very weird and wonderful!

TUTTI POLE - adjacent Bridge 84. Coffees, lunches and teas in quaint surroundings. Tel: 01488 682515.

H's - bar and bistro on Church Street. Tel: 01488 681199.

THE BEAR - Charnham Street (north of Bridge 84) Tel: 01488 682512. Well appointed old hotel offering bar and restaurant food. Elizabeth I and William of Orange have stayed here, and you should have seen the bill for their mini-bars.

HUNGERFORD GOURMET ORIENTAL TAKEAWAY - High Street. Tel: 01488 686898.

THE DOWN GATE - Park Street. Charming pub on the edge of Hungerford Common, well worth a 15 minute walk. Tel: 01488 682708. Arkells ales from Swindon and a good choice of food.

Disappointing in terms of individual food shops, Hungerford has become something of a centre for the antiques trade, BELOW STAIRS (Tel: 01488 682317) up past the railway bridge on the High Street being a typical example of this new focus of commerce. More practically, there is a SOMERFIELD supermarket adjacent to the railway station, whilst if it's time to freshen up your undies, you'll find a handy launderette towards the top of the High Street.

TRAINS - Thames Trains along the Kennet corridor. Tel: 08457 484950.

BUSES - Thamesdown links with Swindon. Tel: 01793 428428 as well as lots of local services along the Kennet Valley. Tel: 01635 567500.

FROXFIELD - where Wiltshire gives way to Royal Berkshire - once boasted a wharf and a feeder. Little remains of the former, but the feeder still enters the canal just below Froxfield Bottom Lock. Bridge 90 offers access to Froxfield village which boasts a remarkable group of almshouses known as the Duchess of Somerset's Hospital.

A change of county brings a change of mood as the A4 trunk road comes alongside the waterway to shake it out of its sleepy complacency. Fortunately, however, much of the A4's traffic has been siphoned off by the parallel M4 and it's not as fearfully busy as it once was. In any case, the K&A maintains its dignity as it makes its unruffled way eastwards accompanied by the River Dun which it crosses on a compact three-arched aqueduct above Cobbler's Lock.

Hungerford Marsh Lock is equipped with a swing bridge across the lock chamber, making it unique on the Kennet & Avon Canal and unusual even on the wider inland waterway system. The bridge was provided for the benefit of the commoners who enjoyed - and for that matter still do - rights over Freeman's Marsh, across which the canal journeys in company with the River Dun and the railway.

Hungerford's canalscape is immensely pleasing, a number of the wharfside buildings having been sympathetically restored for residential use. For well over a hundred years the wharf was occupied by J. Wooldridge & Son, builders, who were also responsible, from 1851-63, for the maintenance of the K&A between Wootton Rivers and Reading. They finally left the site in 1962. The present incumbents are ducks, swans, picnickers and a K&A Canal Trust trip boat.

In tandem with the crystal clear waters of the River Dun, the K&A crosses Hungerford Port Common, where commoners rights were granted by John O'Gaunt, father of King Henry IV, back in the fourteenth century. At Dun Mill Lock, confluence of the Dun and the Kennet, a couple of former mills have been converted into highly desirable residential. See how clear the Kennet is here. Further downstream, as it becomes navigable, turbidity becomes a problem, in other words you can't see the bottom from the top. Anglers believe that this is caused by diesel-powered boats whose propellers disturb the silt and bring an unwelcome opacity to the water that inhibits weed growth and affects fish stocks. It would be sad if this proved true.

PRECONCEPTIONS that the best scenery belongs to the K & A west of Hungerford, and that it continues to get better the further you travel, are belied by the beauty of the Kennet's watermeadows. This is a mouthwatering length of navigation, as tasty as the watercress once grown in the extensive beds bordering the waterway between Hungerford and Kintbury, and punted downstream for onward transportation by rail. The cress farm has long since disappeared - overwhelmed by competition from the large growers in Hampshire and Dorset - and this is now the territory of the solitary angler and towpath walker.

Travelling eastbound, canal users encounter the capricious currents of the River Kennet for the first time. It was at Kintbury in June 1797 that the first section of the K&A was officially opened by its then chairman Charles Dundas, who was present to greet a military band transported along the cut from Newbury specifically for the jollifications. For a hundred years or so Kintbury Wharf thrived,

handling large quantities of iron and coke destined for several local ironworks, as well as raw materials for the nearby brewery. Following the canal's commercial decline and subsequent restoration, Kintbury took centre stage again in December 1972 when Miss W. Rennie, a descendant of John Rennie, officially reopened Kintbury Lock.

Untroubled by the outside world, the canal glides cheerily along in a world of its own, past the sublime slopes of The Wilderness and Irish Hill. The latter was once the site of a curious industry, chalk from the hill being gathered for the manufacture of whiting, a powder used in the production of paint. There were at one time five whiting mills in the Kintbury area, which sent their finished products along the canal to Bristol until the 1930s.

Those familiar with the music of Gerald Finzi might find it entering their heads. Finzi lived at Ashmansworth to the south of Newbury and founded the Newbury String Players during the Second World War. His very measured and lyrically English compositions inevitably find a resonance amidst the beauty of the Kennet Valley and its watermeadows.

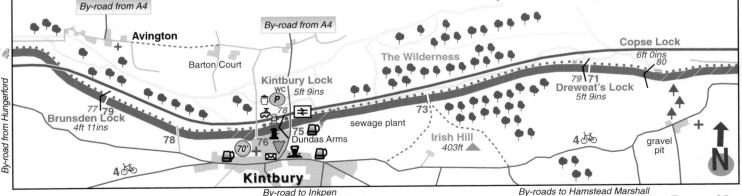

HE Newbury Bypass, once the most infamous stretch of road in Britain, finally opened for business in November 1998, sixty two years after it was first mooted. The eight miles of new road took three years to build, cost a staggering £100 million (plus 10,000 ancient and mature trees) and resulted in the arrest of 1,014 people, including protesters, private security guards and contractors. The net effect of the bypass has been to cut journey times between the South Coast and the Midlands by an average of five minutes, whilst the volume of traffic in Newbury, although reduced in the short term, is expected to return to its pre-bypass level within ten years.

Ponder these facts and figures as you make your way beneath the new road bridge, its impact on the canal emphasised by the scenic splendour of nearby Hamstead Park, Enborne Copse and Benham Broad, the latter being an artificial lake created during the canal's construction to placate the Earl of Craven. But, for the canal traveller at least, the new bypass is but a temporary blot on the landscape and better things lie in store as Newbury reaches out to embrace the K&A. First though you pass beneath the Lambourn Valley Railway bridge, which carried trains of the LVR between Lambourn and Newbury from April 1898 until closure of the passenger service in January 1960. And there you have it - UK transport policy summed up perfectly during a ten-minute saunter along the towpath of the K&A: close railways and build roads.

Newbury is as welcoming as a log fire on a winter's evening. Indeed, it's difficult to think of any other town of comparable size which enhances a canal journey so comprehensively. If you're Reading bound the attractions begin at West Mills, where a swing bridge, a row of picturesque cottages (once a 17th century weaving factory) and the mill's surviving silo

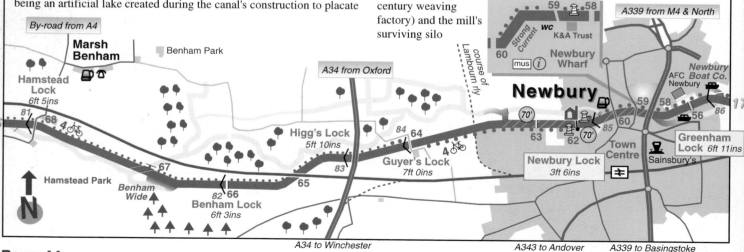

(tastefully converted into flats) combine to create a canalscape of picture postcard beauty. But Newbury hasn't always been the commuter town it is today. It was an important cloth-making centre in the fifteenth century and down the centuries manufacturing and commerce played important roles in the town's development. West Mills Wharf was once a hive of activity, handling, amongst other commodities, coal from the Somerset collieries. Its last commercial use came in 1950 when a cargo of salt from Middlewich was delivered by John Knill.

Newbury Lock was the first to be completed, in 1796, on the Newbury-Bath section of the canal. Unique on the K&A, it is equipped with lever-operated ground paddles of a type relatively common on northern canals, where they are referred to as cloughs. Beside the lock a small plaque, unveiled in 1997, pays tribute to the late John Gould MBE, founder member of the Kennet & Avon Canal Trust and former working boatman, who died in March 1999. "Without him there would be no K&A Canal." Ambushed by the lively waters of the Kennet and a mill stream that enters from the opposite side, the navigation proceeds under Town Bridge - a stylish, single-arched stone structure dating from 1770. Being the terminus of the original Kennet Navigation, it was built without a towpath, which presented problems for horse-drawn craft, especially as it was forbidden for horses to haul across the main road. The solution involved a special float, kept by the lock; whilst the barge was tied below the bridge and the horse by the lock, the float was attached to the tow rope and allowed to drift down below the bridge to the barge. Then once the horse started pulling the barge would move through the bridge and into the lock. Downstream the natural flow normally being sufficient to carry the vessel through the bridge. Moorings are provided at Victoria Park (although we consider West Mills to be the nicest place to spend the night), directly opposite Newbury Wharf. Originally the terminal wharf of the Kennet Navigation, this was one of the busiest wharves on the K&A, but most of it disappeared under, in chronological order, a bus station, car park and the main Inner Relief road. The two-storeyed Stone Wharf Building survives, however, and serves as K&A Canal Trust branch headquarters, shop and small museum.

Kintbury (Map 15)

A delightful village with a notable church within which a tablet commemorates Charles Dundas, noting that he represented the County of Berks in 'ten successive Parliaments in full possession of every faculty' which is more than can be said of many of us.

DUNDAS ARMS - canalside Bridge 75. Well known waterside inn named after the first Chairman of the Kennet & Avon Company. Tel: 01488 658263. *Two other pubs up in the village.*

How nice to find such a small village supporting a butcher and a baker as well as a newsagent and general store.

TRAINS - local services along the Kennet Valley, *very* useful for towpath walks. Tel: 08457 484950.

Newbury (Map 16)

Few towns successfully embrace the inland waterways on their doorstep as comprehensively as Newbury. The navigation passes through the very heart of the town, whereas most communities tend to keep their distance from so vulgar a hinterland. Northbrook Street, the main shopping thoroughfare, is carried across the navigation enabling a quick shop to be done while your boat is worked through Newbury Lock. Look out for the imposing church of St Nicholas built in the 16th century by a wealthy Newbury wool merchant.

LOCK STOCK & BARREL - Bridge 60. Tel: 01635 42730. Modern Fullers pub with waterside terrace.
HOGSHEAD - Wharf Street. Tel: 01635 569895. CAMRA recommended former auction mart conversion. Wide range of beers, waterside patio.
DESMOULIN - adjacent Newbury Wharf. Tel: 01635 35001. Very pleasant cafe adjunct to art gallery. Soups, pasties, quiches and pies.

An enjoyable town to shop in with all facilities very close to the canal. Don't miss the opportunity to purchase some Newbury Sausage from GRIFFINS butchers overlooking Bridge 60.

TOURIST INFORMATION - The Wharf. Tel: 01635 30267.
WEST BERKSHIRE MUSEUM - The Wharf. Tel: 01635 30511. Excellent local museum housed in former cloth hall and granary.
BUSES - contact Newbury Buses on 01635 567500.
TRAINS - Thames Trains offer excellent services along the Kennet Valley. Tel: 08457 484950.

GREENHAM has its bridge, its island, used for moorings by the Newbury Boat Company, its lock and its mill, once an important cloth mill before being sold in 1903 to a company who supplied Newbury with electricity. It once had a wharf too, subsequently buried beneath the police station, where the 109 foot long, 110 ton 'Newbury' barges were built. Gradually, time is erasing Greenham's synonymy with nuclear missiles and it's all too easy to forget the mass protests and the Women's Peace Camp, all of which was acted out less than a mile south of the K&A.

The railway masks Newbury's famous racecourse and heads for open country. A strange kind of country it is too, a mix of water meadows and marshland, once the site of extensive osier beds. Osier is a species of willow used in basket-work. Today the area north of the canal is an important ecological site where reed and sedge warblers and rare butterflies thrive in a unique lake and reed bed environment; the Nature Discovery Centre, located close to Widmead Lock, offers the chance to explore this fascinating terrain along a number of designated paths.

At just over a mile, the Long Cut is the longest straight on the entire K&A. The cut leads on to Monkey Marsh Lock, ostensibly one of the last remaining examples of the turf-sided locks once prevalent on the Kennet Navigation. These had timber walled chambers to some two feet above the lock's lower level, above which their turf sides sloped away at an angle of 45 degrees. Whilst the locks were filling there was considerable water loss through the turf banks but copious supplies of water from the Kennet meant that this was not considered a problem. Sadly, Monkey Marsh Lock has been inappropriately restored with copious use of concrete and steel, an ugly compromise, leaving one to suspect an excess of health and safety considerations.

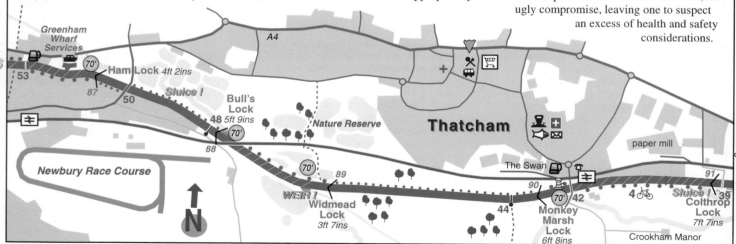

LOW-LYING, yet well-wooded, the navigation exudes great charm as it continues its undemonstrative way through the Kennet Valley. To the north, Bucklebury Common rises to over four hundred feet; to the south Crookham Common is almost as high: both form rewarding horizons.

The railway remains a constant companion, its passenger expresses and locals leavened by lengthy goods trains carrying Wiltshire-quarried stone to the construction company stockpiles of Greater London. Incidentally, the Great Western Railway years ago renamed the little station on Woolhampton's doorstep 'Midgham', concerned lest Woolhampton be confused with Wolverhampton, the Black Country industrial centre north of Birmingham!

Swing-bridges abound: No.31, at Woolhampton, deserves care and attention when approached from upstream as, below the tail of the lock, the river makes a brisk entrance, and you must have your wits about you if you are not to be the cause of merriment (at best or *schadenfreude* at worst) amongst the patrons of the adjoining beer garden. Electrified now, the bridge poses no inherent problems in operation, but reflect that, in 1940, Tom and Angela Rolt took three hours to negotiate their way past

the bridge with the help of 'half the able-bodied men of the village heaving on crow-bars under the direction of the red-faced landlord of the Row Barge. On the same journey, the locks were in equally recalcitrant condition, and the Rolts were grateful for an abundance of reeds, bunches of which they heaved into the lock chambers to staunch the flow of water from heavily leaking gates.

An earlier traveller and writer to explore the K&A had been Fred S. Thacker, whose book *Kennet Country* was published by Blackwells of Oxford in 1932. He and his wife voyaged along the navigation in 1919, even then not without difficulty, both mechanical and bureaucratic: 'It has cost me some weeks of negotiation with the railway company, and an initial outlay of twenty shillings to obtain a permit to enter the Kennet.'

Halfway along the picturesquely wooded interlude between bridges 30 and 29, the Kennet leaves the canal and heads off in the direction of Aldermaston, being navigable, for those of a curious disposition, at least as far as Frouds Bridge Marina, if not Aldermaston Mill which once received its grain by barge.

Thatcham *(Map 17)*

A lengthy walk through suburbia faces the canal traveller intent on visiting the fleshpots of Thatcham. Closer at hand, however, is a good pub, whilst a few minutes further on are a row of shops providing most of life's necessities (paracetamol and fish & chips for example). But if you feel like stretching your legs, Thatcham does evince a curious post Sixties charm about its town square. Almost the only building left of any antiquity is the church, though even that was 'violently restored' in 1852 according to Betjeman & Piper's *Architectural Guide to Berkshire*. A Millennium monument in the square salutes some of Thatcham's significant events, such as the arrival of electric light in 1920, the first telephone in 1912, and the Kennet Navigation in 1723, whilst, in 1160, Thatcham Market was attacked by a band of brigands from Newbury. Stirring stuff!

SWAN HOTEL - Station Road. Tel: 01635 862084. Food and accommodation. *More pubs in the town centre, plus Thatcham seems to have more fish & chip shops than a northern mill town, the nearest being just 5 minutes walk from Bridge 42. Also in the town centre are several ethnic restaurants and takeaways.*

There's an 'Alldays' general stores within 5 minutes of the canal as well as a pharmacist and post office. All the main high street banks have branches in the town centre where you'll also find a Waitrose supermarket, a Co-op and even a small bookshop. Best of all, however, is WYATTS butchers & fishmongers shop - Tel: 01635 863241 - a real find.

BUSES - Newbury Buses link the town centre with Newbury and Reading. Tel: 01635 567500. *Services 1/2 offer a 30 minute* frequency connection between the railway station and the town centre.

TRAINS - Thames Trains services to/from Newbury and Reading with useful stops at Midgham and Theale for towpath users. Tel: 08457 484950.

Woolhampton *(Map 18)*

Former coaching village on the old Bath Road, suffering demolition when the road was widened. Douai Abbey can be accessed to the North.

ROW BARGE - canalside, Bridge 31. Tel: 0118 971 2213. Convivial freehouse with beer garden overlooking the navigation. Food, families welcome.

FALMOUTH ARMS - Bath Road (village centre) - Tel: 0118 971 3202. Friendly local offering food, families welcome. B&B.

THE ANGEL - Bath Road. Beautifully appointed restaurant which may dent your plastic but with a concomitant rise in morale. Tel: 0118 971 3307.

Post Office stores which sells newspapers - open daily, mornings only on Sundays. Well stocked garage shop on A4 to east.

TRAINS - Thames Trains. Remember the station's called 'Midgham' ! Tel: 08457 484950.

Aldermaston Wharf *(Map 19)*

Aldermaston itself lies a country mile to the south-west along the A340 but the wharf itself is worth lingering over and you should start with British Waterways' VISITOR CENTRE (Tel: 0118 971 2868) which was originally a canal employee's cottage. A short waymarked trail will introduce you to Aldermaston Wharf's salient features including: the former transhipment arm, the lock, the lift- bridge, and the remains of an old brewery. Refreshments and gifts are also available at the visitor centre.

BUTT INN - a few hundred yards south of the canal at Aldermaston Bridge. Tel: 0118 971 2129. Bar meals, families welcome, garden.

TRAINS - Thames Trains. Local services linking Newbury with Reading. Tel: 08457 484950.

Theale *(Map 19)*

Quainter than Thatcham, and not such a long walk from the canal, Theale has a friendly air about it and an adequate choice of shops. Its church is an imposing example of Gothic revival which includes interior work by Bodley, very much worth a visit by aficionados of church architecture.

CUMBERS - High Street. Tel: 0118 930 2405. Succulent hot sandwiches etc to take-away. *Lots of pubs and Thai and Chinese restaurants also.*

Co-op, pharmacy, newsagent, post office, bakery and Lloyds TSB bank all located on the High Street seven or eight minutes stroll from the canal at Bridge 19.

TRAINS - Thames Trains linking local stations along the canal between Reading and Newbury. Tel: 08457 484950.

SILICON chip business parks may embower the A4, but the Kennet & Avon keeps its head down, remaining remote and unruffled, marching past Aldermaston Wharf in its own silent protest at progress and man's inhumanity, not so much to man, as to the landscape.

Long before the era of the nuclear protest marches, the Great Western Railway inserted an arm off the main channel of the canal to facilitate interchange between rail and water. It paralleled the railway for some distance but most of it was infilled at the outset of the Second World War - doubtless some top brass tactician foresaw the Third Reich commandeering the arm to further its strategic advance across southern Britain. We may scorn from the sophistication of the 21st century, but fear makes fools of us all, and are we not equally irrational now in the face of terrorism? Try finding a litter bin at a railway station and you have the answer.

In point of fact, the military identified the K&A as a Blue Defence Line. Pill boxes were installed at numerous locations. According to Rolt: 'The last of the Kennet & Avon boatmen was dragged from retirement and put in charge of a leaking maintenance boat hauled by a broken-down horse led by a dim-witted youth'. Ere long, the vessel, overloaded by inexperienced squaddies, sank and put a summary end to the proceedings. Our good friend, George Behrend (author of that peerless railway book *Gone With Regret*) recalls tank practice in the vicinity of the canal, and an altercation with a senior officer who refused to accept that the average K&A swingbridge was not necessarily designed to bear the weight of a tank.

Researching this length one wintry day, we came upon horses splashing through floodwater in fields neighbouring the navigation like something out of the Camargue. Even in monochrome, and with foreshortened horizons, we could sense how beautiful the K&A could be. Ufton Lock has disappeared. It was only shallow in any case, a mere 1ft 9ins, provided in the 1830s to give greater depth below Towney Lock. Towney was rebuilt as part of the restoration programme in 1974, and associated improvements rendered Ufton obsolete.

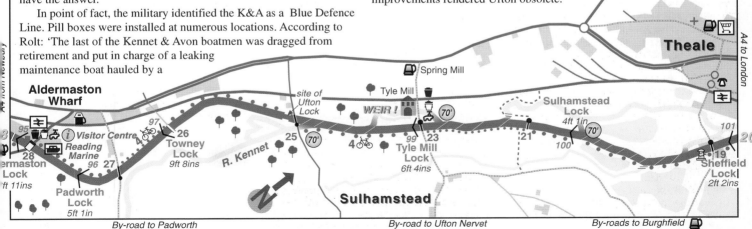

Aldermaston Wharf · Visitor Centre · Reading Marine · 95 · 28 · Aldermaston Lock 11ins · 96 · 27 · Padworth Lock 5ft 1in · 97 · 26 Towney Lock 9ft 8ins · R. Kennet · 25 · site of Ufton Lock · 70' · Spring Mill · Tyle Mill · WEIR! · 70' · Tyle Mill Lock 6ft 4ins · 99 · 23 · Sulhamstead · By-road to Padworth · By-road to Ufton Nervet · Sulhamstead Lock 4ft 1in · 21 · 100 · 70' · 101 · Theale · A4 to London · 19 Sheffield Lock 2ft 2ins · 20 · By-roads to Burghfield

*T*HE M4 motorway impinges briefly. You can marvel at its ugliness. One day it will be grass-grown, nothing is more certain. And then we will love it, wondering at the romance of its heyday.

As for the K&A you will be either conscious of its impending end or coming slowly to terms with its prosaic beginnings in a gravel pit flawed landscape. Keep the faith, back in 1919 Fred S. Thacker slaked his thirst at the Cunning Man (whose landlord didn't know the source of its name) discovered 'alluring lanes' leaving for Binfield, Grazeley and Shinfield and quickly learnt that a voyage along the Kennet 'is very delightful'.

Garston Lock is essentially (see Map 17) the sole remaining turf-sided chamber and one can't help thinking that the pillboxes overlooking it are there to protect it from Progress. At Bridge 17 the towpath changes sides and the National Cycle Route No.4 detours off to the south, passing former gravel workings now adopted by Theale Water Skiing Club. Burghfield Lock - and, indeed, all the original twenty turf-sided locks between Reading and Newbury - originally dates from between 1715

and 1724, but was enlarged in the 1760s to accept the massive 'Newbury' barges which measured 19ft in the beam and 109ft in length and could carry a cargo of over a hundred tons. The lock chamber in use now dates from the early years of restoration and was ceremoniously opened by the Chairman of British Waterways in 1968.

There were osier beds beside the canal between bridges 15 and 14. They were once harvested for basket making. Burghfield Island provides popular private moorings away from the main navigable channel under the aegis of the Burghfield Island Boat Club. Downstream of Southcot Lock the railway line from Reading to Basingstoke crosses the navigation. An important link between the midlands and the south, there are frequent Virgin Voyagers and a considerable amount of container traffic making its way to and from Southampton Docks, making one wish there was still a residue of commercial traffic on the Kennet & Avon. Fobney Lock is overlooked by Reading's waterworks and its associated pumping station and filter beds.

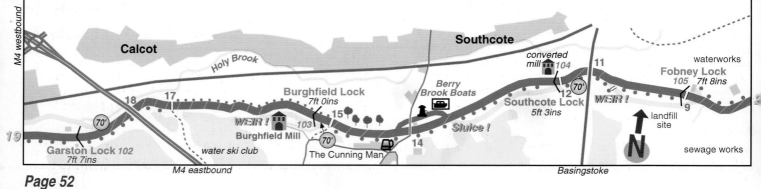

READING forms the pivotal point in this guidebook. Here we exchange the regal Thames for the rather less celebrated, though hardly less charismatic Kennet & Avon or vice versa. The two waterways' passage through the county town of Berkshire could hardly be more contrasting: the Thames wide and spacious, the Kennet hemmed in by an urban backdrop and a new high tech retail zone. By most standards, however, this retail park, known as 'The Oracle' makes successful use of the navigation, incorporating it to a higher degree than most other examples we have met on our inland waterway travels: from the glass fronted House of Fraser cafe, Reading's shoppers regard passing boaters with jaw-dropping awe, perhaps in the sudden realisation that retail therapy can't compete with canal travel in the final analysis.

Eastbound, County Lock is the last under British Waterways' jurisdiction, boaters proceed under traffic light control from here owing to the narrow nature of the channel ahead, one-way operation being the order of the day. The strength of the current is often increased by the narrow nature of the channel, westbound you may notice that your boat is making heavy weather of its progress; eastbound, don't get carried away!

Simonds Brewery overlooked the Kennet from 1789 onwards until the business was bought out by Courage in 1960 and, typically, closed a dozen years later. The navigation here was known as the 'Brewery Gut', and it was both deep and dangerous. As at Newbury, the absence of a towpath made difficult working practices for horse-drawn barges. At one point a line was attached to a pulley and the boat horse given a sharp smack on its hindquarters which had the effect of propelling the barge in to the bridgehole. Further on a long length of rope was floated down the navigation and attached to the barge, which had to be hauled a further two hundred yards from the bank. Ponder on these archaic working practices as you watch juggernauts unloading at the rear of the retail centre. Yes, we've come a long way, but so much has been lost in the process.

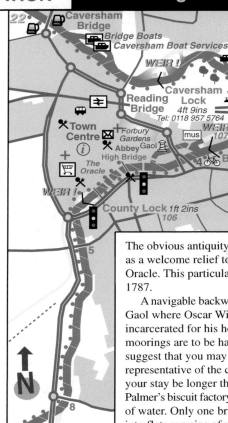

The obvious antiquity of High Bridge comes as a welcome relief to the modernity of The Oracle. This particular structure dates from 1787.

A navigable backwater loops past Reading Gaol where Oscar Wilde was famously incarcerated for his homosexuality. Good moorings are to be had here, though notices suggest that you may be approached by a representative of the council for a fee should your stay be longer than 4 hours! Huntley & Palmer's biscuit factory overlooked this stretch of water. Only one brick building converted into flats remains of what was in its heyday a 24 acre site. The new Prudential Building occupies much of this, a landmark symbolic of industrial change. Up until the Second World War water transport was used both to bring flour in to Huntley & Palmers and take finished biscuits out, many destined for morale-boosting export to outposts of the empire via London Docks.

Blakes Lock is operated by the Environment Agency and evinces all the characteristics of a Thames lock. Licences can be purchased from the keeper for use of the Thames and/or the Kennet & Avon if your boat is not already so equipped.

Gasholders and railway bridges mark the confluence of the Kennet with the Thames. Not the most romantic of backdrops, but adrenaline is likely to be running in any boater or walker making the transition - it always does at inland waterway junctions, whatever their nature. For such a large town, Reading lets its river off lightly, respecting its integrity and not allowing urbanisation to compromise matters, for once one does not necessarily find oneself in accord with Jerome K. Jerome's opinion that the river at Reading is 'dismal and dirty'. Reading Bridge and Caversham Bridge span the Thames as it skims the northern edge of the town and Caversham Lock needs to be negotiated. Fry's Island plays host to two hire bases and a bowling club whose 'Bohemian' members have to make use of a private ferry to gain access to their greens.

Reading (Map 21)

In common with Northampton perhaps, Reading tends to be thought of as a County Town that is superficially uninspiring. In both cases nothing could be further from the truth. Squeezed between the Thames and the Kennet, Reading exudes brash overtones of London, but manages to retain the atmosphere of Berkshire. Should one slacken one's gait on Broad Street, the main thoroughfare, one is pestered by beggars, religious zealots and market researchers with the assiduousness of merchants in a kasbah. Avoid eye contact at all cost, lift up your gaze instead to the terracotta embellishments of Reading's Edwardian shops, and seek out the quieter oases of calm as manifested by Forbury Gardens (where the Mainwand Lion commemorates members of the Berkshire Regiment lost in the Afghan War of the 1880s) and the Abbey ruins. Two churches deserve notice: St Laurence-in-Reading and St Mary the Virgin, the latter with a chequerboard tower of flint and limestone. In the 18th century Wiltshire stone was carried down the Kennet to build a crescent reminiscent of Bath on Queen's Road which runs parallel to the south of the canal east of High Bridge.

LONDON STREET BRASSERIE - High Bridge. Tel: 0118 950 5036. Stylish modern restaurant with terrace overlooking the navigation.
NINO'S - Market Place. Tel: 0118 958 8966. Lively Italian restaurant.
LOCH FYNE - Fobney Street (opposite county Lock). Tel: 0118 918 5850. Seafood restaurant and bar. Breakfasts, lunches and dinners.
JE T'AIME - Friar Street. Tel: 0118 951 3151. Inexpensive French bistro.
FISHERMAN'S COTTAGE - Kennet Side (by Blakes Lock). Tel: 0118 957 1553. Food and Fuller's beer in convivial canalside pub.
THREE MEN IN A BOAT - Caversham Bridge. Tel: 0118 925 9988. Restaurant & bar adjunct to Holiday Inn Hotel. Riverside terrace.
PIPERS ISLAND - Caversham Bridge. Tel: 0118 948 4573. Pavilion like bar on the Thames. Food, families welcome.
HOBGOBLIN - Broad Street. Tel: 0118 950 8119. CAMRA recommended serious drinker's den.

Bookended by Debenhams and the House of Fraser, THE ORACLE offers 21st century shopping, but you know our sympathies lie elsewhere. Come with us to Union Street (alias 'Smelly Alley') where FROSTS the fishmongers and DUDMANS the 'high class' greengrocers and GILBERTS the butchers ply their trade and you will not be disappointed. KEEGANS secondhand bookshop lurks on Merchants Place off Friar Street.
TOURIST INFORMATION - Church House, Chain Street. Tel: 0118 956 6226.
BLAKES LOCK MUSEUM - Gasworks Road. Tel: 0118 939 0918. Reading's social and industrial history housed in a former sewage pumping station. Highly recommended!
MUSEUM OF READING - Town Hall. Tel: 0118 939 9800. Housed in Alfred Waitresses's imposing town hall of 1875. Must see!
TRAINS - services along the Thames and Kennet valleys. Tel: 08457 484950.
BUSES - Tel: 0870 608 2608.

DESPITE the proximity of the main line railway and the strung out suburbs of Tilehurst, the Thames retains its integrity, unimpeachably lovely however we care to compromise it. Reading is rapidly shaken off when travelling upstream, in the opposite direction it delays showing its urban hand until the last possible moment.

The Thames Path detours through the suburban environs of Purley, an incongruous excursion for serious walkers caused long ago by the obduracy of a local landowner who refused even the powerful Thames Commissioners access on to his meadowlands. As a result the towpath changed banks and two ferries plied back and forth with boat horses and pedestrians; naturally neither survive.

Rolling hills and woods characterise the view to the north. The environs of

MAPLEDURHAM LOCK - the first Thames lock to be mechanised in 1956 - are outstandingly scenic, arguably the Thames's finest. Mapledurham House is of 16th century origin and is widely considered one of England's finest Tudor buildings. It was home to the Catholic Blounts, a secret tunnel leads to the adjoining church. Royalists used secret rooms and passages within the house during the Civil War. John Galsworthy wrote the final chapters of his *Forsyte Saga* whilst staying in the house and E. H. Shepard who illustrated *The Wind in the Willows*, is said to have been inspired by the setting. The adjoining watermill has been restored and is open to the public at set times. At one time its power was harnessed to provide the house with electricity. Hardwick House is even older than Mapledurham. Elizabeth I stayed here and Kenneth Grahame is thought to have modelled Toad Hall on it.

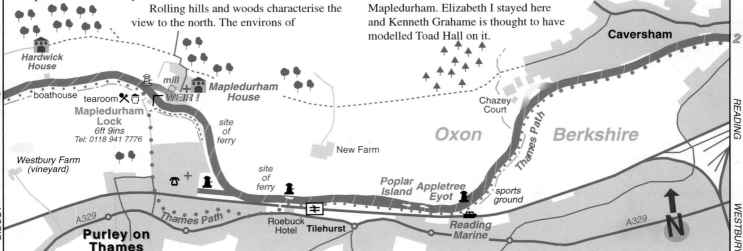

IT does not come as any great surprise to learn that Kenneth Grahame, who wrote the incomparable children's classic, *The Wind in the Willows*, spent a good deal of his life in Pangbourne and was inspired in telling the story to his young son by the river scenery of his own boyhood. You too will fall for the beauty of these reaches of the Thames and, like Mole, be 'intoxicated with the sparkle, the ripple, the scents and the sounds and the sunlight'.

Whitchurch Toll Bridge is made of iron and was built in 1902. Sensibilities alter with time, for Eric de Mare, the photographer, architectural writer and close friend of L. T. C. Rolt proclaimed the bridge 'no beauty' in his book *Time on the Thames* published in 1952. Fifty years later, in its centenary year, its whitewashed span gleams appealingly below the lock, and by modern standards looks anything but ugly, and it is the hard-hearted motorist who begrudges his ten pence to cross such a characterful structure in such a gorgeous setting. Incidentally, the only other toll bridge on the

Thames is at Swinford, some half dozen miles upstream of Oxford, which currently costs just five pence to negotiate, perhaps because the river is narrower!

Briefly, beyond Pangbourne and Whitchurch, the Thames path detours away from the riverbank, any disappointment incurred is amply compensated by being reunited with the river amidst the beech and yew tree and chalk cliff setting of Hartslock Wood, the name of which recalls the existence of a former lock in the neighbourhood.

Forming the boundary between Berkshire and Oxfordshire, the river makes attractive progress through a gracious landscape full of historical and natural interest. In the churchyard at Lower Basildon Jethro Tull, the agriculturist who gave his name to a Sixties rock band, is buried. Beale Park wildlife centre is home to many rare breeds and endangered species. Pangbourne Meadows belong to the National Trust. The tiny River Pang enters the Thames shyly, having risen on the Berkshire Downs south of Didcot.

The Millstream, Whitchurch, River Thames

Peaceful moorings at Pangbourne, River Thames

Pangbourne *(Map 23)*

A row of elegant late Victorian houses which line the riverbank to the west of Pangbourne are known as the 'Seven Deadly Sins'. Lady Cunard, the socialite, was once a resident here, and these houses set the rather racy tone for a likeable little town marred only by a surfeit of road traffic. Public moorings are to be found on the Berkshire bank downstream from Whitchurch Toll Bridge. To reach the centre on foot you must negotiate a constricted tunnel under the four track railway. Kenneth Grahame lived at Church Cottage and when he died the church was decorated with fresh willows in honour of his famous book.

THE SWAN - riverbank, moorings for customers. Tel: 0118 984 4494. Famous old Thameside inn fondly remembered as the spot where the Three Men and Montmorency shamefacedly abandoned their boat and caught the train to Paddington. Bar and restaurant meals, families welcome.

MIA BENI - town centre Italian restaurant just through the railway bridge. Tel: 0118 984 4440.

COPPER INN HOTEL - Church Road. Tel: 0118 984 2244. Bar and restaurant meals and accommodation.

LINA TANDOORI - town centre. Indian takeaway. Tel: 0118 984 5577.

LAUGHING HALIBUT - town centre. Fish & chips. Tel: 0118 984 1614.

Several attractive looking cafes and pubs as well.

A good collection of shops make Pangbourne a useful base. There are branches of the big four banks, a small Somerfield supermarket, a branch of W.H. Smith, a butchers, a pharmacy and a handy launderette near the station.

BEALE PARK - lovely wildlife sanctuary with moorings for visitors by boat. Tel: 0118 984 5172. www.bealepark.co.uk

BASILDON PARK - Tel: 0118 984 3040. 18th century Palladian mansion designed by John Carr (of York) for a man who made a fortune in India. Now operated by the National Trust and accessible from the west bank of the river at Lower Basildon.

TRAINS - frequent Thames Trains along the river corridor. Tel: 08457 484950.

BUSES - Thames Travel service 139 links Benson with Wallingford, Goring, Pangbourne and Reading. Tel: 01491 874216.

Whitchurch-on-Thames *(Map 23)*

Peaceful and shopless, the picturesque houses of Whitchurch cling to a steep hill on the Oxfordshire bank of the Thames. Two pubs offer refreshment to walkers on the Thames Path: The Ferryboat (Tel: 0118 984 2161) and The Greyhound (Tel: 0118 984 2160).

Goring *(Map 24)*

Perhaps the quintessential Thameside village, Goring has been the scene of an annual regatta since 1887. Good moorings below the bridge offer easy access to quaint streets where the use of flint and timber is prevalent. The Norman church boasts one of the oldest bells in Britain. Walkers on The Ridgeway and Thames Path may doff their hats to each other as they cross the river.

RIVERSIDE - Bridge Approach. Tel: 01491 872243. Tea room and takeaways.

THE MILLER OF MANSFIELD - High Street. Tel: 01491 872829. Bar and restaurant meals.

CATHERINE WHEEL - Station Road. Charming CAMRA recommended pub. Tel: 01491 872379.

RAJPUT - High Street. Indian restaurant & takeaway. Tel: 01491 872796.

JOHN BARLEYCORN - Manor Road. Tel: 01491 872509. Brakspear ales, food & accommodation.

LEATHERNE BOTTLE - Cleeve. *Closed for refurbishment as we went to press.*

You wouldn't necessarily find a village in the midlands and north with such a good choice of shops: three banks, a post office, butcher, off licence, pharmacist, gift shop and a dealer in teddy bears. All these, however, pale in comparison with W.H. NAPPER a superbly old fashioned grocers shop and general store and conduit of local gossip - Tel: 01491 872626.

TRAINS - Thames Trains to/from London, and Oxford. Tel: 08457 484950.

BUSES - Thames Travel service 132 links Goring with Benson and Reading via Wallingford and many other river villages. Tel: 01491 874216.

Streatley *(Map 24)*

Odd how each river crossing throws up neighbouring communities where the economy of one has thrived at the expense of the other's. In this case Streatley is the shy, retiring type and many would remark all the more appealing for it, and indeed there are some charming brick buildings in the vernacular Thames Valley style.

SWAN DIPLOMAT - highly regarded riverside hotel open to non-residents. Beautiful waterside gardens with an Oxford College barge permanently moored alongside. Tel: 01491 873737. Al fresco meals in summer.

THE BULL - Reading Road. Nice old pub at the top of the village. Food & families welcome. Tel: 01491 872507.

NEVER a dull moment as the Thames flows purposefully through the Goring Gap, an Ice Age leftover between the Berkshire Downs and The Chilterns. Walkers have to decide which pathway suits them best: the Thames Path upstream of Streatley hugging the west bank, The Ridgeway the east. Sadly the old ferries at Little Stoke and Moulsford no longer function, so crossing the river and combining the paths into circular walks is not a ready option. Moulsford ferry was immortalised anonymously by H. G. Wells in his delightful novel *The History of Mr. Polly*, which, by virtue of the chapter called 'The Potwell Inn' alone, deserves its niche in the pantheon of Thames inspired literature. Apparently Wells stayed at the Beetle & Wedge Inn whilst engaged on the book. Alfred Polly, who found convivial employment as the ferryman, would not recognise the inn now, for it has become smart and orientated in the general direction of fine cuisine, but his memory lingers affectionately on in the minds of ferry enthusiasts.

Moulsford Railway Bridge was originally the work of Isambard Kingdom Brunel and as such dates from 1840. When the line was quadrupled fifty years later, a second span was added on the downstream side, linked to the older bridge by curious little cross arches.

Cleeve Lock is approached from downstream past a maze of islets and backwaters. The pound between the locks at Goring and Cleeve is the shortest on the river, whilst, strangely, that between Cleeve and Benson is the lengthiest.

Goring Bridge carries both The Ridgeway and the Thames Path across the river, its length necessitated by the weir channel and the millstream, a quintessential Thames scene of great charm. Oscar Wilde once lived in the old Ferry Cottage which later became the home of 'Bomber Harris', the controversial architect of Britain's blanket bombing raids on Germany.

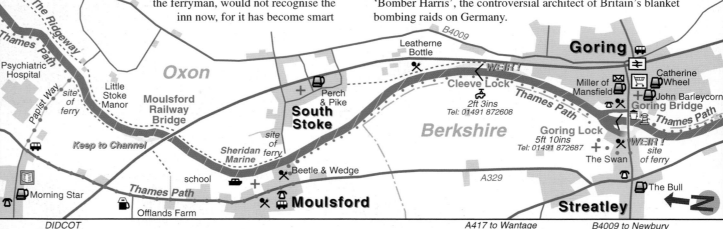

THE Thames moves at a more sedate pace than its 21st century hinterland. Journeying on or beside it offers the opportunity to fall back through the years to what we now perceive as a gentler era of canvassed camping skiffs and meadowland picnics. Wallingford hardly impinges on this spell. Its bridge boasts seventeen arches, though only five span the river. There is a charge for mooring overnight upstream on the town side of this bridge - downstream the far bank is gratis. One imagines the town council consider £5 for vessels of less than 35 feet and £8 for anything over a reasonable price to pay, though it is significant that upstream at Abingdon the municipal moorings come free of charge.

RAF Benson dates from 1937 and will forever be associated with de Havilland 'Mosquitos'. During the Second World War these aircraft had sufficient range to reach the Balkans. During the war Benson was home of the Photographic Reconnaissance Unit. Nowadays it remains a vibrant base for Merlin and Puma helicopters.

Though their attitude to boaters differs, Wallingford and Abingdon were firmly against the advent of the Railway Age, both spurning Brunelian advances to bring the Great Western Railway to their doorstep. The ensconced self-interest of river traders may have had a bearing on this hostility, but it did result in isolation from the march of 19th century commerce and industry. Eventually both towns lowered their guard and linked themselves umbilically to the main line, but too late for their shortlived branches, closed to passengers respectively in 1959 and 1963, to rouse their towns out of their historic torpor.

South of Winterbrook Bridge, which carries Wallingford By-pass across the Thames, the Thames Path is joined by The Ridgeway, the two National Trails hugging their respective riverbanks as far as Streatley. The Ridgeway runs from Avebury in Wiltshire to Ivinghoe Beacon in Hertfordshire, a distance of eighty-five miles.

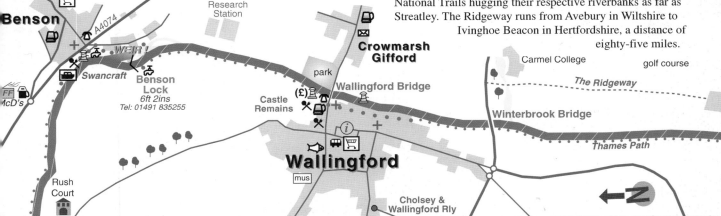

South Stoke (Map 24)

Idyllic village isolated from the outside world by the river and the railway. The 13th century church notable for its glass. Other buildings use tile, thatch, flint and weatherboarding to much effect. Suitable moorings for a visit by the old ferry staithe.

PERCH & PIKE - village centre. Tel: 01491 872415. Really lovely village pub offering food and accommodation.

Moulsford (Map 24)

A corruption of 'Mules Ford'. The church is the work of George Gilbert Scott and lies hidden between the road and the riverbank. The inn gets its name from tools used in wood cutting; a 'beetle' being a heavy type of mallet. As well as being associated with H.G. Wells, another literary guest was George Bernard Shaw.

BEETLE & WEDGE HOTEL - Ferry Lane. Tel: 01491 651381. Sophisticated eating establishment offering a choice of restaurants. OLD BAKERY -on A329. Tel: 01491651589. Informal restaurant.

Cholsey (Map 24)

The Great War poet, Edward Thomas, crossed the Thames by ferry from Little Stoke to Cholsey and walked up the Papist Way while researching on foot his book *The Icknield Way*. In the bar of the Morning Star he eavesdropped as a drayman and a butcher's boy agreed that motor-cars were ruining the roads. What prescience, for this was 1912! Agatha Christie is buried in the isolated churchyard beyond the railway.

Wallingford (Map 25)

The prehistoric origins of 'Walling ford' are self explanatory. Alfred the Great fortified the town against the Danes and William the Conqueror erected a castle here. It dominated the town for five hundred years and in the 12th century supported Queen Matilda against King Stephen. When decay set in, Henry VIII ordered much of its timber and lead to be shipped downstream for enlarging Windsor Castle. Nowadays Wallingford wears such history lightly and is fun to perambulate. Work outwards from the Tourist Information Centre housed in the old Town Hall and you won't go far wrong.

THE BOATHOUSE - riverside by Wallingford Bridge. Bar & grill. Tel: 01491 834200.
WALLINGFORD TANDOORI - High Street. Tel: 01491 836249.
NELLO'S - High Street. Italian restaurant. Tel: 01491 835500.
GEORGE HOTEL - High Street. Tel: 01491 836665. Bar & restaurant meals in a nicely appointed hotel.
THE DOLPHIN - St Mary's Street. Nice little town pub, food and accommodation. Tel: 01491 837377.

Wallingford is a pleasant place to shop in with a Waitrose supermarket and a full range of banks. Friday is market day and there's a launderette on High Street within easy reach of the river. TOBY ENGLISH'S secondhand bookshop on St Mary's Street usually has an excellent selection of Thames related material.

TOURIST INFORMATION - Market Sq. Tel: 01491 826972.
WALLINGFORD MUSEUM - High Street. Tel: 01491 835065. Open Mar-Nov,Tue-Fri afternoons, Saturdays 10.30-5pm. Also Sundays Jun & Aug.

Cholsey & Wallingford Railway - Tel: 01491 835067. Short preservation train rides on 'The Bunk'.

BUSES - from the Market Square buses run to Oxford and Reading and the nearest railhead at Cholsey. Tel: 01491 874216.

Benson (Map 25)

Also occasionally known as Bensington, Benson is chiefly known for its RAF base these days, though a couple of centuries ago it was an important staging post for coaches on the Oxford to Henley run. The centre of the village lies across the busy A4074.

THE WATERFRONT - versatile and egalitarian riverside cafe/restaurant. Tel: 01491 833732.
THE CROWN INN - High Street. Old coaching inn offering food and accommodation. Tel: 01491 838247.

Newspapers, gifts and limited groceries available from a shop adjunct to the cafe. Otherwise you'll have to walk into the village centre (taking care of the traffic) where you'll find a small Somerfield supermarket, a butcher, a pharmacy, a post office and a newsagent.

BUSES - useful links for walkers with Wallingford and Abingdon. Tel: 01491 837988.

Shillingford (Map 26)

The wharf here used to serve a long gone brewery and goods were discharged for the larger village of Warborough to the north. Now all is peace. Look out for the flood level markings on an adjacent wall and be thankful you weren't hereabouts on the 27th January 1809 !

Continued on page 66

I N some circles - albeit ever decreasing ones - the Thames above its confluence with the confusingly named Thame is known as Isis. This River Thame, navigable as far as Dorchester by the intrepid crews of diminutive vessels, rises to the east of Aylesbury, close to the Grand Union Canal. Its name derives from an eponymous market town on the north-eastern border of Oxfordshire notable in that the eccentric restaurateur John Fothergill once kept the Spread Eagle there. But our focus remains resolutely on the Thames, dominated visually hereabouts by the Sinodun Hills, alias Wittenham Clumps, little more than three hundred feet above sea level, though positively mountainous in the context of the Thames flood plain. L.T.C. Rolt thought of this as the reach of the river which most appealed to him. Moor either side of Day's Lock,

and make it your business to explore Little Wittenham Nature Reserve, lovingly tended by the Northmoor Trust. Waymarked trails lead through the woods or to the top of Round Hill and Castle Hill from which there are prodigious views and remnants of Iron Age fortifications. From these superior viewpoints more visual sense can be made of the Dyke Hills on the east bank of the river above Day's Lock, another example of ancient defences.

Shillingford Bridge, graceful, dating from 1827 and marking the halfway point between Reading and Oxford, is overlooked by an hotel with a riverside open air swimming pool. A number of handsome boathouses stand beside the river; one, adjacent to Shillingford Court, has a picturesquely thatched roof.

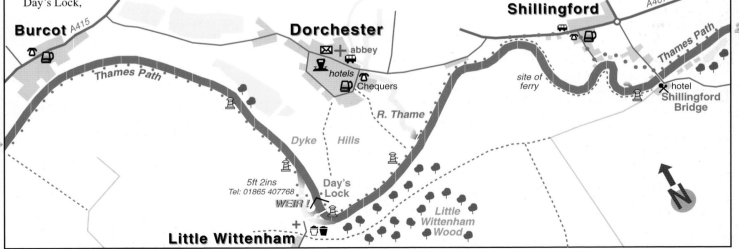

Continued from page 64

SHILLINGFORD BRIDGE HOTEL - riverside. customer moorings. Tel: 01865 858657. Comfortable three star hotel offering bar and restaurant food to non residents.

THE KINGFISHER INN - Henley Road. Tel: 01865 858595. Food and accommodation. 5 minutes walk from the river.

Dorchester *(Map 26)*

Not to be confused with Thomas Hardy's Dorchester, Dorchester-on-Thames (and surely that should be Dorchester-on-*Thame* !) is a gloriously sleepy place, by-passed (relatively recently) by the main road and by-passed, it appears, by time itself. O-level historians will realise, given the second syllable of its name, that it boasts Roman origins. Accessible from moorings above or below Day's Lock - from which a footpath leads across the prehistoric mounds of the Dyke Hills - the centre is dominated by a Decorated Abbey approached through a Butterfield lych gate and justly renowned for its astonishing Jesse window.

CHEQUERS - Bridge End. The first pub you encounter tempts you to go no further. Beer comes from the cellar, there's no piped music, and food is refreshingly restricted to rolls and sandwiches. In short, a gem ! Tel: 01865 340015.

THE GEORGE HOTEL - High Street. This three star hotel was originally a coaching inn and can trace its history back to the 15th century. Tel: 01865 340404.

THE WHITE HART - High Street. Ditto above. Tel: 01865 340074.

CHESTERS - Queen Street. Quaint tea rooms. Tel: 01865 341467.

FLEUR DE LYS - High Street. 16th century pub. Tel: 01865 340502.

Well known as a centre for antiques, Dorchester's practical shopping is restricted to a small Co-op store and a post office.

ABBEY MUSEUM - Tel: 01865 340751. Small museum devoted to local history and the abbey. Open May-September, Tuesday-Saturday 11am-5pm and Sundays 2pm-5pm.

BUSES - Thames Travel Service 139 links Dorchester with Wallingford and Abingdon. Tel: 01491 874216.

Clifton Hampden *(Map 27)*

"Self-consciously picturesque" avowed John Piper in his 1938 *Shell Guide to Oxfordshire*, and you can still see what he meant. Sergeant William Dykes who accidentally began the Battle of Waterloo is buried in the churchyard. Post office stores.

BARLEY MOW - riverside. This famous and popular inn ('the quaintest, most old-world inn up the river' according to JKJ) is now part of the Chef & Brewer chain. MG used to use its picturesque appearance as a backdrop for their publicity shots. Tel: 01865 407847. Moorings on opposite bank.

Long Wittenham *(Map 27)*

Backwaters always beguile, and moorings to the rear of The Plough offer every inducement to turn temporarily away from the main channel to explore the low-lying village of Long Wittenham. The predominantly Early English church is very pretty. Robert Gibbings, the engraver, and author of *Sweet Thames Run Softly*, who spent his last years in Long Wittenham, is buried in the graveyard. Another erstwhile resident of renown and vision was Roye England the model maker and founder of the Pendon Museum who arrived

here in 1954 and converted the old Three Poplars pub into a Youth Hostel.

THE PLOUGH - High Street. Tel: 01867 207738. An attractive village pub offering bar and restaurant food, families welcome, bed & breakfast.

THE VINE - High Street. Tel: 01865 407832. Equally nice looking pub as above. Also in the village, tucked away down a lane, you'll come upon the curiously named Machine Man Inn.

Post office stores adjacent to Pendon Museum.

PENDON MUSEUM - 'museum' is a misnomer, Pendon houses an extraordinary 1:76 model of the Vale of the White Horse *c*1930s which has taken the best part of fifty years to build and work continues. Other exhibits include a railway running at the edge of Dartmoor and John Ahern's brilliant Madder Valley Railway. Absolutely not to be missed! Open 2-5pm Saturdays and Sundays and also Wednesdays in July and August. Tel: 01865 407365.

BUSES - Thames Travel services. Tel: 01491 837988 or 874216.

Sutton Courtenay *(Map 27)*

An embarrassment of fine buildings characterises this quiet village on an un-navigable backwater. Unfortunately it is some distance on foot from the nearest moorings on Culham Reach. That small point apart, however, should not dissuade you from visiting Sutton, the pools are utterly picturesque and Eric Blair (aka George Orwell) is buried towards the bottom right corner of the churchyard. There are three fine pubs, notably THE FISH, a Les Routiers recommended inn noted for its seafood menu. Tel: 01235 848242.

Clifton Hampden Bridge, River Thames

Abingdon

Course of Abingdon Railway

Nuneham Railway Bridge

28

26

Town Centre

Kingcraft

WEIR !

Abingdon Lock 6ft 2ins
Tel: 01235 523044

WEIR !

WEIR !

Salters Steamers

Abingdon Bridge

Andersey Island

Abingdon Town F.C.

Swift Ditch

R. Ock

Wilts & Berks Canal

Abingdon Sailing Club

A415

Clifton Hampden

Clifton Hampden Bridge

Barley Mow

Clifton Lock 3ft 5ins
Tel: 01865 407821

Clifton Cut

BARELY two miles separate the railway bridges which span the Thames at Nuneham and Appleford though by water it's almost five miles, so that two minutes train travel is prolonged into a couple of hours by boat. But who's counting? En route the river encounters Abingdon, reputedly its prettiest riverine town, and no true explorer could begrudge the Thames its elaborate wanderings, yet consider that the navigable distance would be great still were it not for the 'cuts' at Clifton and Culham, though, paradoxically, the main channel originally by-passed Abingdon by way of Swift Ditch.

Three locks punctuate the boater's stately progress and the countryside is never less than charming. Some may consider the railway bridges ugly, but such aesthetes will find ample consolation in the road bridges at Abingdon, Sutton and Clifton, the last the work of Sir George Gilbert Scott.

The Lion

Culham

P

Culham Lock 7ft 11ins
Tel: 01235 522061

Sutton Bridge

Culham Cut

Thames Path

Appleford Railway Bridge

WEIR !

The Plough

The Vine

B4016

WEIR !

The Fish

Sutton Courtenay

mus

Pendon Museum

Long Wittenham

Appleford

DIDCOT

N

Between 1810 and 1906 Abingdon was the junction for the Wilts & Berks Canal (see also Map 6) its main trade being in Somersetshire coal and local agricultural produce, although, ironically, it does prove useful in the movement of materials for construction of the Great Western Railway through the Vale of the White Horse. Unlike the Kennet & Avon, it was a narrowbeam canal, and this restriction certainly did it no favours with the advent of the Railway Age. Trade at the Abingdon end had all but evaporated in the 1880s and there is virtually no trace of the canal's junction with the Thames other than a slight indentation in the retaining wall above Wilsham Road, close to where the River Ock joins the main river beneath a little iron bridge bearing the misleading inscription: 'Wilts & Berks Canal 1824'. Abingdon might have become an inland waterway crossroads if the plan for a canal to Aylesbury had ever come to fruition.

Clifton Cut dates from 1822, and Culham Cut from 1809. Prior to their construction trade was hampered by flash locks and the use of the river by a watermill at Sutton Courtenay. Swift Ditch probably represented the original course of the river before Abingdon's monks diverted the channel past their abbey. In the 17th century Swift Ditch regained its importance as the main line of navigation and featured one of the earliest pound-locks in England. Around 1790, with the construction of a lock at Abingdon, Swift Ditch lost its status and became a backwater once again.

Appleford Railway Bridge dates from 1843 and its construction led to much debate between the Thames Commissioners and the Great Western Railway whose line approached the river from either direction on low-lying ground. A high bridge to facilitate the passage of masted vessels would have necessitated lengthy approach embankments which would have been detrimental to high speed running. The railway builders appear to have had things their way, for the bow span girder bridge stands only thirteen feet above water, the third lowest crossing on the whole river below Oxford.

Abingdon (Map 27)

Rationalisation, that clouded mirror image of enterprise, has rid Abingdon of its Morland Brewery and MG sports car plant, yet such sadnesses notwithstanding, the 'Queen of the Thames' remains an engaging town full of architectural, cultural and historical surprises. Pearsons would not be Pearsons, though, if we did not take umbrage at Abingdon's post 1974 transfer from Berkshire to Oxfordshire, the crass meddling of politicians and bureaucrats overturning the stabilities of centuries - reorganization for reorganization's sake. That off our chests, we commend Abingdon to you and suggest that you see the remains of the Abbey, St Helen's high-spired, flying-buttressed church, and the amazing County Hall, a Wren-like building which has been declared 'the grandest town hall in England' .

BROAD FACE - Bridge Street. Tel: 01235 524516. Immensely appealing eating establishment close by Abingdon Bridge. Highly recommended.
UPPER REACHES - Thames Street. Hotel offering meals to non residents immediately upstream of bridge. Tel: 01235 522311. Moorings for patrons.
NAG'S HEAD - Bridge Street. Pub on the bridge with nice garden overlooking both the navigable channel and the backwater from which Salters' steamers depart. Tel: 01235 536645.
PUNCH BOWL - Market Place. Tel: 01235 520230. 16th century drinking den in the shadow of the wondrous County Hall. Morland ales, alas no longer brewed in the town but in Bury St Edmunds.

A good place to shop if, in our opinion, not quite so rewarding as Wallingford. A modern precinct leads from the Market Place and provides just about everything one might need without resorting to supermarkets.

TOURIST INFORMATION - Bridge Street. Tel: 01235 522711.
ABINGDON MUSEUM - County Hall, Market Place. Tel: 01235 523703. Worth visiting just to be in the beautiful building which houses it. Copious displays of local history. Exhibits relating to MG who built their cars in Abingdon from 1929 until 1980, during which time over a million models were made, 75% of which were exported to America! Access to the roof top balcony on Saturdays in summer.

BUSES - Oxford Bus Co. service X3 offers a frequent daily link between Abingdon and Oxford city centre and railway station. Services 32A & 35A operate southwards to Didcot Parkway railway station. Tel: 01865 785400.

PERHAPS even the Thames itself would admit to being at its most lacklustre between Iffley and Abingdon. In the reach below Sandford Lock especially it is characterised by accompanying scrubland and a plethora of electricity pylons. But these are minor lapses in concentration and quickly forgiven. Elsewhere on this stretch there is much to look out for and muse over. Kennington Railway Bridge carries the rump of the old line via Thame to Princes Risborough, and over it now - instead of a Prairie tank and a pair of superannuated carriages - run goods trains bearing Minis, freshly made at the motor works in nearby Cowley. This is *Progress* we're assured. Another victim of time has been the paper mill at Sandford Lock, its former site occupied by housing now.

Narrowboats used to bring coal down from the Warwickshire coalfield to feed its hungry furnaces. Sandford, with an almost nine foot fall, is the deepest lock upstream of Teddington. Its origins can be traced back to 1632. In contrast, the lock-keeper's cottage dates from 1914.

Downstream of Radley College boathouse, shallow hills and woods redeem the anodyne reach above. Nuneham House overlooks the river and in its gracious grounds stands the Carfax Conduit, an artefact pertaining to Oxford's 17th century water supply rendered redundant by the widening of High Street in 1787. Not a great deal can be seen from the river of the house itself (in which Victoria and Albert honeymooned in 1841) but the grounds are the work of no lesser a gardener than 'Capability' Brown. Lock Wood Island recalls the existence of a lock at this point which ceased being used around 1800, at which time the channel changed from the east side to the west.

A4074

Sainsbury

Sandford on Thames

hotel

King's Arms

former mill

WEIR !
Sandford Lock
8ft 10ins
Tel: 01865 775889

Thames Path

rowing club

Nuneham House

Carfax Conduit

Lower Radley

Lock Wood Island

Kennington Railway Bridge

Kennington

Radley College

Radley rly sta

DIDCOT

OXFORD

27 Page 71

TOWN and Gown may define the City of Oxford's personality split, but the gulf is echoed by its canal and its river: the former self effacing and humdrum, the latter exhibitionist and haughty. Access between these contrasting inland waterways is by way of the Sheepwash Channel, spanned by the main railway line into Oxford from the north and overlooked by new housing. Upstream the Thames remains navigable as far as Lechlade, a delightful route earmarked for coverage in the Severn, Avon & Cotswold Canal Companion.

Via Osney Lock the Thames traverses the western periphery of Oxford, re-encountering the railway and passing beneath a sturdy bridge of iron construction which once carried a siding into the gasworks - even the Thames can be mundanely functional when duty calls.

But for most residents and visitors the Thames at Oxford manifests itself most obviously at Folly Bridge where punts are available for hire and Salter's faded yet still elegant 'steamers' can still be taken throughout the summer season at least as far as Abingdon.

One wonders if it's the undergraduates or the tourists who take to punting nowadays, it seems too sentimental an activity for modern youth. Yet the college rowing clubs obviously continue to flourish, even if their stately barges have been for the most part replaced by club houses with a firm grasp of terra firma. With your gaze attracted by these sizeable establishments you might miss the gentle ingress of the Cherwell, Oxford's most ethereal watercourse. More business like, the Thames negotiates the typically picturesque Iffley Lock, already establishing, for downstream newcomers, its capacity for escaping the less salubrious aspects of its mundane hinterland.

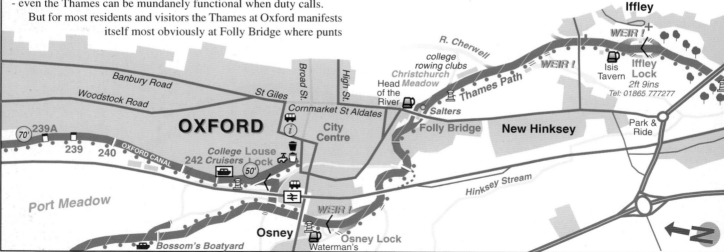

Oxford (Map 29)

Oxford's pressures seem not so much 'Town & Gown' nowadays, as 'Town & Tourism'. Yet it can still remind you of an exclusive club, where the best the casual visitor can do is press their nose up against the lattice windowpane and peer enviously at the academically privileged world revealed within. Like Thomas Hardy's hero, we are all 'Obscure Judes', in awe of this world-renowned seat of learning. In Oxford - perhaps more than in any other English city - time stands quite literally still. Whole quadrangles and cloisters seem frozen into a medieval eternity where only the undergraduates ubiquitous bicycles break the chronological spell. From the perspective of the river boat, or the open-topped tourist bus, the sightseer can derive a vicarious wisdom. After all, you can now truthfully recall: "When I was at Oxford."

ISIS TAVERN - riverside above Iffley Lock. Tel: 01865 247006. Isolated yet popular riverside inn which used to have its beer delivered by barge. Moorings nearby.
HEAD OF THE RIVER - Folly Bridge. Tel: 01865 721600. Lively conversion of former grain warehouse. Waterside terrace.
WATERMANS ARMS - riverside above Osney Lock. Tel: 01865 248832. Cosy local, bar food.
LAMB & FLAG - St Giles. Ancient inn associated with C.S. Lewis and Tolkien and, in recent years, one Endeavour Morse. Lunchtime food. Tel: 01865 515787.
THE NOSEBAG - St Michael's Street. Tel: 01865 721033. Long established wholefood cafe/restaurant.
FISHERS - St Clements. Close to Magdalen Bridge. Fish and seafood restaurant. Tel: 01865 243003.
LIVEBAIT - The Turl. Tel: 01865 324930. Contemporary seafood restaurant.
BROWNS - Woodstock Road. Tel: 01865 319655. Well established brasserie converted from former Morris garage.
LE PETIT BLANC - Walton Street. Tel: 01865 510999. Raymond Blanc owned restaurant hidden away in the backstreets of Jericho.
RESTAURANT ELIZABETH - St Aldates. An Oxford institution, predominantly French cooking. Tel: 01865 242230.

Drawing on a wide range of custom and taste, Oxford's shops are inspired to an admirable eclecticism. The COVERED MARKET (off High Street) hosts the most wonderful cross-section of retailers and those who have travelled the length and breadth of this guide from Bristol will find a resemblance to the market there. As befits a seat of learning, there are some good bookshops, though not, sadly, as many secondhand and antiquarian outlets as we seem to remember.

TOURIST INFORMATION - The Old School, Gloucester Green. Tel: 01865 726871. Assemble here for guided walking tours relating to many aspects of Oxford.
GUIDE FRIDAY - open top bus rides with running commentary. Regular departures from the railway station and city centre stops. Tel: 01865 790522.
THE OXFORD STORY - Broad Street. Jorvik style ride through Oxford's rich history. Tel: 01865 728822.
MUSEUM OF OXFORD - St Aldates. Tel: 01865 815559.
ASHMOLEAN MUSEUM - Beaumont Street. Tel: 01865 278000. Britain's oldest public museum (not Mons) displaying European, Egyptian and Near Eastern antiquities.
CARFAX TOWER - Carfax. 99 steps to heaven for a bird's eye view of the city of dreaming spires.
PUNT HIRE - Oxford's most traditional means of seduction can be hired from boat houses at Folly Bridge on the Thames and Magdelan Bridge on the Cherwell.
COLLEGES - over thirty colleges make up Oxford University. Many of them are world famous such as Balliol and Merton which are both of 13th century origin; Magdalen (pronounced 'Maudlin') which dates from 1458; and Christ Church founded in 1525 by Cardinal Wolsey. The general public may look around most of them in the afternoons.
OPEN SPACES - much of Oxford's charm rests in the proliferation of green spaces, the city's lungs. These include: The Parks, Christ Church Meadow and Port Meadow. A stroll - or a picnic - on any of them comes as a refreshing experience after the hurly burly of the main thoroughfares and helps put Oxford in the context of its riverside setting.

TRAINS - services along the Thames Valley to/from Reading and London and connections to/from the midlands and the north. Tel: 08457 484950.
BUSES - contact the Oxford Bus Company on 01865 785400.

Sandford-on-Thames (Map 28)

KING'S ARMS - Sandford Lock. Popular riverside pub offering bar and restaurant meals. Families welcome. Tel: 01865 777095.
THE FOX - Henley Road. Tel: 01865 777803. CAMRA recommended unspoilt village pub serving Morrells though it is no longer brewed in Oxford.

How to use the Maps

There are twenty-nine numbered maps whose layout is shown by the Route Planner inside the front cover. Maps 1 to 21 cover the Kennet & Avon between Bristol and Reading; Maps 21 to 29 cover the River Thames between Reading and Oxford. The maps are easily read in either direction. The simplest way of progressing from map to map is to proceed to the next map numbered from the edge of the map you are on. Figures quoted at the top of each map refer to distance per map, locks per map and average cruising time. An alternative indication of timings from centre to centre can be found on the Route Planner. Obviously, cruising times vary with the nature of your boat and the number of crew, so quoted times should be taken only as an estimate. Neither do times quoted take into account any delays which might occur at lock flights in high season or against strong current conditions on the river sections.

Using the Text

Each map is accompanied by a route commentary, and details of most settlements passed through are given close by. Regular readers will already be familiar with our somewhat irreverent approach. But we 'tell it as we find it', in the belief that the users of this guide will find this attitude more valuable than a strict towing of the tourist publicity line.

Towpath Walking

The simplest way to go canal exploring is on foot. It costs largely nothing and you are free to concentrate on the passing scene; something that boaters are not always at liberty to do. The towpath on the Kennet & Avon Canal is in good condition throughout, though at times of flood sections may be impassible between Hungerford and Reading. The Bristol Avon is provided with a towpath for much of its length, though on one or two occasions it is necessary to detour away from the riverbank. The famous Thames Path is a 180 mile long distance path following the river from its source in Gloucestershire to the Thames Barrier in East London. Between Reading and Oxford it mostly follows the old towing path except for one or two places where former ferries have ceased to function

making detours necessary. In the course of preparing this guide we have walked every yard of the K&A, Avon and Thames towpaths ourselves and can thoroughly recommend them as a means of getting to know these inland waterways without a boat. As usual the maps show the quality of the towpath, and whilst it does vary from area to area, none of it should prove problematical for walkers.

Towpath Cycling

Cycling canal towpaths is an increasingly popular activity. At present it is theoretically necessary for cyclists wishing to use towpaths to acquire a free of charge permit from a British Waterways office - see opposite page for appropriate addresses. Much of the Kennet & Avon towpath is utilised as National Cycle Route No.4 and the surface has for the most part been enhanced with this in mind. Cycling beside the Avon and Thames rivers is not formally encouraged, and the surface of their riverbank towpaths is often unsuitable for bicycling with any degree of comfort. Where appropriate, we have listed cycle hire facilities.

Boating

Boating on inland waterways is an established, though relatively small, facet of the UK holiday industry. There are over 20,000 privately owned boats registered on the canals, but in addition to these numerous firms offer boats for hire. These range from small operators with half a dozen boats to sizeable fleets run by companies with several bases.

Most hire craft have all the creature comforts you are likely to expect. In the excitement of planning a boating holiday you may give scant thought to the contents of your hire boat, but at the end of a hard day's boating such matters take on more significance, and a well equipped, comfortable boat, large enough to accommodate your crew with something to spare, can make the difference between a good holiday and an indifferent one.

Traditionally, hire boats are booked out by the week or fortnight, though many firms now offer more flexible short breaks or extended weeks. All reputable hire firms give newcomers tuition in boat handling and lock working, and first-timers soon find themselves adapting to the pace of things 'on the cut'. Turn to page 78 for contact details of boat hire operations.

Navigational Advice

LOCKS are part of the charm of inland waterway cruising, but they can be potentially dangerous environments for children, pets and careless adults. Use of them should be methodical and unhurried, whilst special care should be exercised in rain, frost and snow when slippery hazards abound. We lack space for detailed instructions on lock operation: trusting that if you own your own boat you will, by definition, already be experienced in canal cruising; whilst first-time hire boaters should be given tuition in the operation of locks before they set out. The locks included in this guide are all of the widebeam variety and capable of accepting two narrowboats side by side. On the Kennet & Avon Canal they are boater operated. Similarly on the River Avon, though usually there are keepers on duty at Netham and Hanham locks. On the River Thames all the locks are mechanised and manned. Their telephone numbers appear on our maps. We recommend boaters on the Thames acquire a copy of the Environment Agency's *A User's Guide to the River Thames*.

MOORING on the canals featured in this guide is per usual practice - ie on the towpath side, away from sharp bends, bridge-holes and narrows. An open bollard symbol represents visitor mooring sites, either as designated specifically by British Waterways or, in some cases, as recommended by our personal experience or that of our regular correspondents. Of course, one of the great joys of canal boating has always been the opportunity of mooring wherever (sensibly) you like. In recent years, however, it has become obvious that there are an increasing number of undesirable locations, particularly in urban areas, where mooring is not recommended for fear of vandalism, theft or abuse.

CLOSURES (or 'stoppages' in canal parlance) traditionally occur on the inland waterways between November and April, during which time most of the heavy maintenance work is undertaken. Occasionally, however, an emergency stoppage, or perhaps water restriction, may be imposed at short notice, closing part of the route you intend to use. Up-to-date details are normally available from hire bases. Alternatively, British Waterways provide a recorded message for private boaters, the number to ring being: 01923 201402. Information is also available on BW's internet site at www.british-waterways.org

Useful Contacts

BRITISH WATERWAYS
The Locks, Bath Road, Devizes, Wiltshire SN10 1HB Tel: 01380 722859.
British Waterways operate a central emergency telephone service - Tel: 0800 4799947.

RIVER THAMES
Environment Agency, Kings Meadow House, Kings Meadow Road, Reading RG1 8DQ Tel: 0118 953 5000.

BRISTOL HARBOUR
Underfall Yard, Cumberland Road, Bristol BS1 6XG
Tel: 0117 903 1484.

The Inland Waterways Association was founded in 1946 to campaign for retention of the canal system. Many routes now open to pleasure boaters may not have been so but for this organisation. Membership details may be obtained from: Inland Waterways Association, PO Box 114, Rickmansworth WD3 1ZY. Tel: 01923 711114. Fax 01923 897000.

The Kennet & Avon Canal Trust was formed in 1962 with the object of restoring the canal to full navigation. You can join the Trust by contacting them at: Kennet & Avon Canal Trust, Devizes Wharf, Couch Lane, Devizes, Wilts SN10 1EB. Tel: 01380 729489.

The Association of Canal Enterprises was founded in 1982 to promote greater use of the Kennet & Avon corridor. It supports many of the businesses who gain their livelihood from the canal. It can be contacted by telephone on 01635 42884.

Acknowledgements

Keith Goss commenced the work on this project and much of the material he produced has been valuably incorporated, all the photographs (unless credited to David Alison or Michael Pearson) are Keith's work; Brian Collings designed and executed the front cover (re-docking it twice as we hovered with uncertainty and a third time when it was 'lost' by an advertising agency); David & Jennifer Alison allowed their holiday boat to be temporarily hijacked by piratical researchers - grateful thanks to them all. Thanks also to Toby Bryant of Central Waterways Supplies, Jackie Pearson, Karen Tanguy and Cristina Negri and all her colleagues at STIGE.

Information 2

Hire Bases with boating facilities

ANGLO WELSH WATERWAY HOLIDAYS - Bristol, River Avon, Map 1. Tel: 0117 924 1200. www.anglowelsh.co.uk

BATH NARROW BOATS - Bath, Kennet & Avon Canal, Map 4. Tel: 01225 447276. www.bath-narrowboats.co.uk

BERRY BROOK BOATS - Burghfield, Kennet & Avon Canal, Map 20. Tel: 07831 574673. www.berrybrookboats.co.uk

BRIDGE BOATS - Reading, River Thames, Map 21. Tel: 0118 959 0346

THE BRUCE TRUST - boat hire for the disabled from bases at Gt Bedwyn (Map 13) and Foxhangers (Map 8). Tel: 01672 516441. www.brucetrust.org.uk

CAVERSHAM BOAT SERVICES - Reading, River Thames, Map 21. Tel: 0118 957 4323.

COLLEGE CRUISERS - Oxford, Oxford Canal, Map 29. Tel:01865 554343. www.collegecruisers.com

FOXHANGERS CANAL HOLIDAYS - Devizes, Kennet & Avon Canal, Map 8. Tel: 01380 828795. www.foxhangers.co.uk

KENNET CRUISES - Burghfield, Kennet & Avon Canal, Map 20. Tel: 0118 971 1115.

READING MARINE - Aldermaston Wharf, Kennet & Avon Canal, Map 19. Tel: 0118 971 3666. www.readingmarine.co.uk

SALLY BOATS - Bradford-on-Avon, Kennet & Avon Canal, Map 5. Tel: 01225 864923. www.sallyboats.ltd.uk

SUNSET HOLIDAYS - Limpley Stoke, Kennet & Avon Canal, Map 5. Tel: 01296 749191. www.sunsetholidays.com

SWANCRAFT - Benson, River Thames, Map 25. Tel: 01491 836700.

WESSEX NARROWBOATS - Hilperton, Kennet & Avon Canal, Map 8. Tel: 01225 769847. www.wessexboats.co.uk

WHITE HORSE BOATS - Devizes, Kennet & Avon Canal, Map 8. Tel: 01380 728504.

Boatyards with a range of facilities

BENSON WATERFRONT - Benson, River Thames, Map 25. Tel: 838304

BRISTOL BOATS - Saltford Lock, River Avon, Map 3. Tel: 01225 872032.

BRADFORD MARINA - Bradford-on-Avon, Kennet & Avon Canal, Map 5. Tel: 01225 864562.

BETTER BOATING - Caversham, River Thames, Map 21. Tel: 0118 947 9536.

BRISTOL BOATS - Saltford Lock, River Avon, Map 3. Tel: 01225 872032.

BRISTOL MARINA - Bristol, River Avon, Map 1. Tel: 0117 921 3198.

DEVIZES MARINA - Devizes, Kennet & Avon Canal, Map 8. Tel: 01380 725300.

FOXHANGERS WHARF - Foxhangers, Kennet & Avon Canal, Map 8. Tel: 01380 828254

FROUDS BRIDGE MARINA - Aldermaston, Kennet & Avon Canal, Map 18. Tel: 0118 971 4508.

GIBSON'S BOAT SERVICES - Honeystreet, Kennet & Avon Canal, Map 10. Tel: 01672 851232.

GREENHAM WHARF SERVICES - Newbury, Kennet & Avon Canal, Map 17. Tel: 01635 31672.

HILPERTON MARINA - Hilperton, Kennet & Avon Canal, Map 6. Tel: 01225 765243.

KINGCRAFT/ABINGDON BOAT CENTRE - Abingdon, River Thames, Map 27. Tel: 01235 521125.

NEWBURY BOAT COMPANY - Newbury, Kennet & Avon Canal, Map 16. Tel: 01635 42884.

PORTAVON MARINA - Keynsham, River Avon. Map 2. Tel: 0117 986 1626.

READING MARINE - Tilehurst, River Thames, Map 22. Tel: 0118 942 3877.

SALTFORD MARINA - Saltford, River Avon, Map 3. Tel: 01225 872226.

SHERIDAN MARINE - Moulsford, River Thames, Map 24. Tel: 01491 652085.

SOMERSET COAL CANAL COMPANY - Monkton Coombe, Kennet & Avon Canal, Map 5. Tel: 01225 722069.

THAMES & KENNET MARINA - Caversham, River Thames, Map 21. Tel: 0118 948 2911.

Day Boat Hire

ANGLO WELSH - Bristol, Avon Navigation, Map 1. Tel: 0117 924 1200.

BATH NARROW BOATS - Bath, Kennet & Avon Canal, Map 4. Tel: 01225 447276. www.bath-narrowboats.co.uk

CAVERSHAM BOAT SERVICES - Reading, River Thames, Map 21. Tel: 0118 957 4323.

DEVIZES MARINA - Devizes, Kennet & Avon Canal, Map 8. Tel: 01380 725300.

DUNDAS ENTERPRISES - Brassknocker Basin, Kennet & Avon Canal, Map 5. Tel: 01225 722292.

KENNET CRUISES - Burghfield, Kennet & Avon Canal, Map 20. Tel: 0118 971 1115.

LOCK INN - Bradford-on-Avon, Map 5. Tel: 01255 868068. www.lockinn.co.uk

SWANCRAFT - Benson, River Thames, Map 25. Tel: 01491 836700.

TRANQUIL BOATS - Semington, Kennet & Avon Canal, Map 9. Tel: 01380 870654.

WESSEX NARROWBOATS - Hilperton, Kennet & Avon Canal, Map 8. Tel: 01225 769847. www.wessexboats.co.uk

WHITE HORSE BOATS - Devizes, Kennet & Avon Canal, Map 8. Tel: 01380 728504.

Trip Boats

BARBARA McLELLAN - trips from Bradford-on-Avon. Tel: 01225 868683.

BRISTOL PACKET - boat trips around the Floating Harbour and on the River Avon. Tel: 0117 926 8157.

FRENCH BROTHERS - boat trips between Wallingford and Goring on the River Thames. Tel: 01753 851900.

JOHN RENNIE - trips along the Kennet & Avon from Sydney Wharf, Bath. Tel: 01225 447276.

JUBILEE - trips from Brassknocker Basin, Monkton Combe. Tel: 01373 813957.

KENNET HORSE BOAT - trips aboard the motor veseel Avon from Newbury Wharf and aboard the horse-drawn vessel Kennet Valley from Kintbury. Tel: 01635 44154.

PEWSEY VALE - public & charter trips from Pewsey Wharf. Tel: 01703 266200.

PRIDE OF BATH - from North Parade Bridge, Bath. Tel: 01225 331647.

ROSE OF HUNGERFORD - boat trips from Hungerford Wharf. Tel: 01488 683389.

SALTERS - scheduled services between Oxford - Abingdon - Wallingford - Reading. Tel: 01865 243421.

Michael Pearson

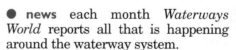